K‍enya

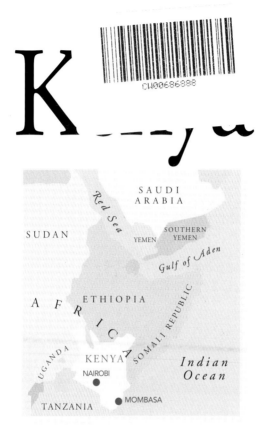

SAUDI
ARABIA

Red Sea

SUDAN

YEMEN SOUTHERN
YEMEN

Gulf of Aden

A   ETHIOPIA

F
R
I
C
A

UGANDA   KENYA

NAIROBI

*Indian
Ocean*

SOMALI REPUBLIC

TANZANIA   MOMBASA

HarperCollins*Publishers*

YOUR COLLINS TRAVELLER

Your Collins Traveller Guide will help you find your way around your holiday destination quickly and easily. It is split into two sections which are colour-coded:

The blue section has the following headings: GAME PARKS, with the parks arranged under subheadings in alphabetical sequence; MOMBASA and NAIROBI, with city attractions followed by excursions from these centres. The topics include information on how to get there, how much it will cost you, opening times and what to expect. Furthermore, there are maps showing the position of each item and the nearest landmark. This allows you to orientate yourself quickly and easily in your new surroundings. To find what you want to do – having dinner, visiting a museum, shopping for gifts or going on an excursion – simply flick through the blue headings and take your pick!

The red section is an alphabetical list of information. It provides essential facts about places and cultural items – 'What is the Rift Valley?', 'Who was Louis Leakey?', 'Where is Hell's Gate?' – and expands on subjects touched on in the first half of the book. This section also contains practical travel information. It ranges through how to find accommodation, where to hire a car, the variety of eating places and food available, tips on health, information on money, which newspapers are available, how to find a taxi and where the youth hostels are. It is lively and informative and easy to use. Each band shows the first three letters of the first entry on the page. Simply flick through the bands till you find the entry you need!

All the main entries are also cross-referenced to help you find them. Names in small capitals – NAIROBI – tell you that there is more information about the item you are looking for under the topic on Nairobi in the first part of the book. So when you read 'see NAIROBI' you turn to the blue heading for NAIROBI. The instruction 'see A-Z' after a word lets you know that the word has its own entry in the second part of the book. Similarly words in bold type – **Wildlife** – also let you know that there is an entry in the A-Z for the indicated name. In both cases you just look under the appropriate heading in the red section.

Packed full of information and easy to use – you'll always know where you are with your Collins Traveller Guide!

CONTENTS

BLUE SECTION

INTRODUCTION   6

GAME PARKS   Aberdare Nat. Park   15
                  Amboseli Nat. Park   19
                  Masai Mara Reserve   23
                  Mt Kenya Nat. Park   29
                  Samburu Reserve   31
                  Tsavo Nat. Park   33

MOMBASA   Restaurants   37
                  Shopping   39
                  What to See   41
                  Excursion 1 North   43
                  Excursion 2 Lamu   49
                  Excursion 3 South   53

NAIROBI   Nightlife   57
                  Restaurants   59
                  Shopping   61
                  What to See   63
                  Excursion 1 Nat. Park   65
                  Excursion 2 Karen   67
                  Excursion 3 Naivasha/Nakuru   71
                  Excursion 4 Western Kenya   75
                  Excursion 5 Lake Turkana   81

CONTENTS

RED SECTION

Aberdares, Accidents & Breakdowns, Accommodation, Adamson, Airports, Amboseli, Arab Influence — 90-92

Baby-sitters, Best Buys, Bicycle & Motorcycle Hire, Bird-watching, Blixen, Budget, Buses — 92-95

Cameras & Photography, Camping, Car Hire, Charter Aircraft, Chemists, Children, Climate, Coffee, Complaints, Conversion Chart, Crime & Theft, Currency, Customs, Customs Allowances — 95-102

Dentists, Disabled People, Drinks, Driving, Drugs — 102-103

Eating Out, Eldoret, Electricity, Eliye Springs, Embassies, Emergency Number, Events, Exploration — 103-107

Fishing, Food, Fort Jesus — 107-110

Gedi, Guides — 110-111

Health, Hell's Gate, Hitchhiking — 111-114

Insurance — 114

Jumba la Mtwana — 114

Kakamega Forest, Kenyatta, Kericho, Kilimanjaro, Kisumu, Kitale — 114-117

Lake Baringo/Bogoria/Nakuru/Turkana/Victoria, Lamu, Language, Laundries, Lost Property, Loyangalani — 117-121

Malindi, Markets, Matatus, Mau Mau, Moi, Mombasa, Money, Mount Elgon/Kenya, Music, Mzima Springs — 121-127

Nairobi, Nakuru, Nanyuki, National Parks & Reserves, Newspapers, Ngong Hills, Nightlife, Nudism, Nyeri — 127-137

Opening Times, Orientation — 137-138

Passports & Customs, Petrol, Police, Post Offices, Public Holidays — 138-140

Rabies, Railways, Religious Services, Rift Valley — 140-141

Safaris, Shopping, Smoking, Sports — 144-145

Taxis, Tea, Telephones & Telegrams, Time Difference, Tipping, Toilets, Tourist Information, Treetops, Tribes — 145-152

Uhuru — 152

What's On, Wildlife — 152-158

Youth Hostels — 158-159

Kenya is, in some senses, a continent in brief. White sands and tropical beaches, ice-capped mountains, humid forests, scorching desert and, of course, abundant wildlife on dry, flat plains. There is something for everyone be they game lovers, adventurers, sun seekers or people watchers.

Kenya spans the equator south of the Sudan and north of Tanzania with Uganda to the west, while the warm waters of the Indian Ocean wash its shores to the east. It is at the heart of what has long been termed East Africa. The climate ranges from temperate in the Central Highlands to

the sunny humidity of the coast and the boiling deserts of the northern frontier.

When you arrive in Kenya one of the first things to strike you is the sheer scale of the landscape. Despite the country's burgeoning population there is a feeling of immense space and wilderness. The country stretches over 582,600 square kilometres of the most diverse landscape found anywhere on the African continent. Mounts Kenya and Kilimanjaro, the two highest mountains in Africa, stand at the centre and on the southern boundary of the country respectively. Elsewhere in the world such impressive snow-covered peaks would still draw attention but here, astride the equator, they are a remarkable sight and it's easy to understand why the first reports of their existence were greeted with scepticism in Europe. But the huge plains filled with an astonishing array of wildlife have to be one of the highpoints of any visit to Kenya. There is little to match the excitement of seeing lion and cheetah at a kill in the cool clear light of an African dawn or the grace of elephant and giraffe wandering slowly across the dusty savanna. After the thrills of a safari the turquoise waters of the Indian Ocean lapping on white sandy beaches lined with palms has to be one of the most peaceful and exotic sounds known to man. But of as much interest as the geography and wildlife of the land are Kenya's people. The sight of Masai *moran* (young warriors) with their spears and ochre-stained hair remains a

daunting and proud spectacle even for the most-travelled of visitors while in the north the presence of ethnic tribespeople in the desolate wastes surrounding Lake Turkana is an awesome reminder of man's adaptability to the harshest of environments. And, of course, despite the impression given by the romantic aura (somewhat manufactured by the entertainment industry) of colonial days, Kenya has a long tribal history proudly reflected in the culture and dress of the individual tribes found in different parts of the country.

In fact, Kenya's history goes back as far as it is possible to go. Some of the oldest remains of man and his ancestors have been discovered within Kenya's boundaries – one skull, found by the famous Louis Leakey, is estimated to be around 2.8 million years old. The Arabs were the first non-African immigrants to arrive, trading with and eventually colonizing areas of the coast. Their influence has proved enduring, as the overtly Islamic atmosphere of Lamu and the Old Town in Mombasa illustrate. Indeed, all of coastal Kenya retains the strong Islamic tradition brought by those 15thC merchants. During the 16th, 17th and 18thC the Portuguese, initially led by Vasco da Gama, contested control of the coastal strip with the Omani Arabs. Ultimately they were to lose the battle although a striking example of their presence can be seen today at Fort Jesus, Mombasa. During the 19thC the British and Germans, the new colonial powers, agreed on areas of control and the stage was set for the complete colonization of Kenya. Primary British concern was not with Kenya at all but with Uganda, for which Mombasa provided the most convenient trading port. It was only as a result of the decision to build a railway from Lake Victoria to the coast that these early colonists came across the rich farmland of the Central Highlands. What became Nairobi had its beginnings as a midpoint staging post for the railway's construction. With its completion came colonists from across the British Empire and Kenya's 'white history' had begun. The early 20thC saw the establishment of huge farms in the area, to the north and west of Lake Naivasha, which was to become known as the 'White Highlands'. While Africans were excluded from the land grants, so building trouble for the future, these first settlers gradually prospered. The period has been amply and evocatively chronicled in books such as *The Flame Trees of Thika*, and films like *Out of Africa* and *White Mischief*. Gradually African grievances grew, particularly at their lack of land rights, and eventually exploded in the early 1950s in the Mau Mau uprising. Members of the Kikuyu tribe attacked the homesteads of white settlers, resulting in a steadily increasing conflict which was to ultimately end in 1960 with over 13,000 Africans and 37 Europeans dead. It was obvious to the British Government that the colonial system had no future in Kenya and three years later, on 12 December 1963, Kenya was granted her independence with Jomo Kenyatta as her first President. Subsequently Kenya has prospered in comparison with many other African states, though poverty and an alarming population growth remain continuing problems. In more recent times there has been unrest over the one-party system of government which prevails in Kenya, most notably marked by rioting and nationwide disturbances in mid-1990. But the people are generally cheerful and hospitable, although you may find street sellers are wise to your attempts to bargain them down. Today there are nearly 20 million Kenyans and it is a truly multi-racial society made up of over 45 tribal groupings plus sizable communities of Asians, Arabs and Europeans. This fertile ethnic mix could be a linguistic nightmare but for the nation's twin common languages of Swahili and English.

Tourism expanded rapidly in the 1980s, a development which has brought with it both benefits and disadvantages. On the plus side Kenya is a considerably more comfortable place to visit than in the past with good-quality accommodation available and a dramatic improvement in roads and communications generally. On the down side the increase in visitors has caused damage to the delicate environment of some of the game parks and has made going on safari a rather busier and less exclusive experience than you might expect. The country is best seen using your own independent transport, allowing escape from the tourist enclaves that have sprung up on the coast and round some of the game lodges. Yet, that said, there is a wide range of tours available that are sensitive to the individual requirements of each visitor. Kenya is a country visitors fall in love with – the stunning landscapes, the thrill of the game drive, the brief but glorious sunsets, and the relaxed, carefree atmosphere draw people back again and again. Long after you've left the smell of dust and wood smoke will stay in your nostrils, the colourful people and their beautiful ever-changing land in your mind. However short, or long, your stay, when you leave you'll feel you need just that little bit longer.

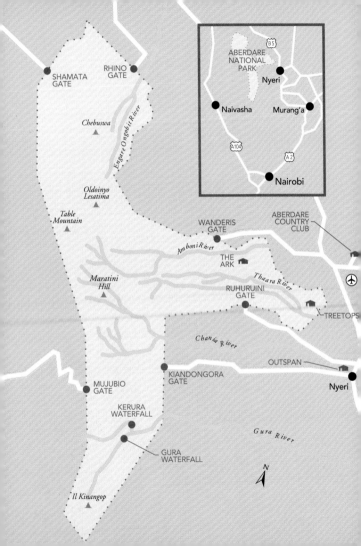

The Aberdare National Park (766 sq. km) lies north of Nairobi atop a 3000 m-high plateau. The Aberdares (see **A-Z**) range of mountains marks the western boundary while to the east the land slopes down to Nyeri (see **A-Z**). At the southern end of the park lie two dramatic water-falls, the Gura, dropping 300 m, and the Kerura. Giant mosses and other vegetation grow round the falls, thriving in the moist atmosphere. Although the climate is often wet and cold there is still a wide range of wildlife in the park, from leopard and lion through buffalo and rhino to the rare bushbuck (*Pongo*) antelope (see **Wildlife**). The thick grass means you have to keep your eyes peeled, though game can often be seen at roadside salt licks.

Perhaps the best and most comfortable way to see wildlife in the Aberdares is the night viewing at the Treetops Hotel (see **Treetops**) and The Ark (see below) where combined water holes and salt licks ensure a nightly parade of elephant, rhino, buffalo and at The Ark, if you are lucky, the black leopard and bongo antelope. For both the Ark and Treetops it is essential to make reservations beforehand, preferably through a tour operator.

HOW TO GET THERE: The park can be reached from the east from Nyeri through any one of three gates, the Ruhuruini, Wanderis or Kiandongora gates. Nairobi approx. 160 km. From the west, on the A 104 from Nairobi to Naivasha, you turn off before Naivasha onto the C 67 signposted to Aberdare National Park and North Kinangop (38 km away). Nairobi approx. 140 km. A steep switchbacking dirt track takes you over the Aberdare mountains to enter the park via the Mujubio Gate. From the north the park can be entered from Nyahururu by either the Shamata or Rhino gates.

WHERE TO STAY: *Lodges* • **Treetops** (see A-Z)**:** visits begin at the Outspan Hotel (see below) where an escort collects you after lunch and returns you next morning for breakfast. Expensive. Water hole, night viewing. No children under ten years old. (Nairobi, tel: 723776.) Princess Elizabeth was staying in the old Tree House Hotel when she acceded to the throne in 1952. Although the original was destroyed by fire, today's rebuilt version remains a fascinating experience. Unfortunately much of the vegetation around the floodlit water hole has been destroyed by elephants.

Treetops

• **The Ark:** visits begin at the Aberdare Country Club (see below) and, as at Treetops, you are collected after lunch and returned for breakfast. Expensive. Water hole, night viewing. No children under seven years old. (Nairobi, tel: 723776.) The Ark is higher in the mountains and, although newer than Treetops, perhaps better designed, offering open and enclosed observation terraces.

• **Outspan Hotel:** near Nyeri. Expensive. Organizes fishing trips. (Nairobi, tel: 335807.) Built round the cottage where Lord Baden-Powell lived, the hotel has wonderful gardens affording brilliant views across to Mt Kenya on clear days. The meals here are excellent.

• **Aberdare Country Club:** north of Nyeri. Expensive. Golf course, swimming pool, tennis courts. (Nairobi, tel: 723776.)

WHERE TO STAY: *Camp sites* Public camp sites are closed as a result of dangerous lions. There are huts at a fishing camp which can be hired. There is also plenty of cheap accommodation in Nyeri.

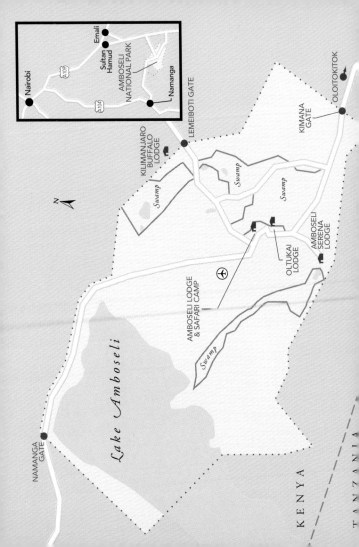

Amboseli Nat. Park

Lying at the foot of Mount Kilimanjaro (see **Kilimanjaro**), the highest mountain in Africa, Amboseli (392 sq. km) has perhaps the most dramatic setting of the Kenyan game parks, with its open plains, and attendant wildlife, overshadowed by the immense snow-capped bulk of the mountain erupting from the bush. Like the Masai Mara (see **GAME PARKS**), Amboseli stands on the Tanzanian border. Lake Amboseli lies at the western end of the park and is usually a dried-out bed of evaporated salts, which acts as a draw for many animals, though it is known to flood in the rainy season.

The park is still used for cattle grazing by the local Masai (see **Tribes**) so don't be surprised to see lone tribesmen and their herds, particularly near the park boundaries. A guide may be advisable in the park as he will know where the animals are most likely to be at any particular time of the year. Off-road driving has caused much damage to the reserve's delicate ecosystem. Visitors should stay on the marked tracks and encourage their drivers to do the same.

Amboseli is particularly known for its large elephant population, although you can see most types of game in the park, particularly in the central and southern sections where animals are attracted by the swamps and water holes. Ostriches can be found on the dry salt flats of the western stretch, grazers and attendant predators in the northeastern grasslands, while in the central and southern swamps you'll find elephant, black rhino and many species of bird (see **Wildlife**).

Sunrise and sunset see Kilimanjaro at its best and most likely to be clear of clouds. Nearby Oloitokitok, beyond the southeastern corner of the park, is worth a visit purely because few other tourists go there. Masai can be seen in and around the village which stands close to Kilimanjaro. The village will give the visitor some insight of life in Kenya, off the tourist trail.

HOW TO GET THERE: There are two roads down to Amboseli from Nairobi. Take the Mombasa road, the A 109, to Athi River (27 km) and turn right onto the A 104 following signs for Namanga and Tanzania. The road then heads south through a burnt-brown rolling landscape for 163 km until you reach Namanga. It is then 80 km to the park centre on a bone-rattling corrugated road, entering via the Namanga Gate. Nairobi approx. 190 km.

Alternatively, take the A 109 Mombasa road and continue through Athi River and onto Emali, 124 km from Nairobi. Here turn right onto the C 102 which runs dead straight for 60 km to Makutano, then turn right and follow signs for the park, past Kilimanjaro Buffalo Lodge to enter the park at the Lemeiboti Gate.

There are daily flights from Wilson Airport (30 min) to the airstrip at Ol Tukai Lodge plus charters to the other lodges from both Nairobi and Mombasa. See **Airports**, **Charter Aircraft**.

WHERE TO STAY: *Lodges* • **Amboseli Serena Lodge:** access via either Namanga or Lemeiboti gates. Located at the southern centre of the park. Expensive. Swimming pool, views onto Engongo Narok Swamp. (Nairobi, tel: 338656.) The accommodation is built to resemble Masai huts, and the veranda and many of the rooms overlook the swamp where elephant and other wildlife may often be seen. Surrounded by vegetation, it is both pleasant and peaceful.

• **Amboseli Lodge & Safari Camp:** access via either Namanga or Lemeiboti gates. Located in the centre of the park. Expensive. Swimming pool. (Nairobi, tel: 338888.) Facing Kilimanjaro, this stone and wood lodge was the first to be established in the park.

• **Kilimanjaro Buffalo Lodge:** access via Lemeiboti Gate. Lies 15 km northeast from the park centre just outside the park boundary and before the Lemeiboti Gate. Moderate. Swimming pool, water hole, airstrip. (Nairobi, tel: 336088.) Attractively designed circular huts, good food and a bar overlooking the water hole for evening viewing.

• **Ol Turkai Lodge:** access via Namanga or Lemeiboti gates. Centre of the park. Inexpensive-moderate. (Nairobi, tel: 331826.) Provides the cheapest accommodation with do-it-yourself huts with toilets, bath, crockery and wood stores. Bring your own food. The lodge was built in 1948 for the filming of Ernest Hemingway's *The Snows of Kilimanjaro*.

WHERE TO STAY: *Camp sites* There is a site 30 km south of Observation Hill (well signposted), but it has no facilities so bring everything. Although outside the park boundary, wildlife can be seen in the area. Book at the Masai Group Ranch on the south boundary.

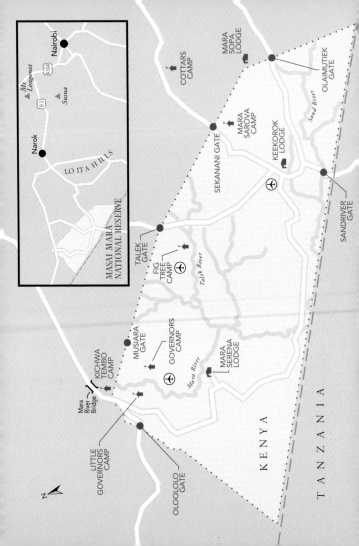

Masai Mara Reserve

The Masai Mara (1800 sq. km) is rated the premier game reserve in Kenya although, in fact, it is merely the northern tip of the Serengeti which extends south into Tanzania. This rolling plain is home to a huge range of wildlife. The visitor can expect to see lion, elephant, hippo, crocodile, wildebeest, cheetah, zebra, giraffe and, with luck, rhino and leopard. The best game is concentrated in the northwest of the reserve, around the Mara River, though expect to see animals everywhere else in the reserve and surrounding lands.

The most spectacular time to visit the Mara is in late June, Aug. and Sep. when a massive migration of some 1.5 million wildebeest and 0.5 million other grazers move north from the Serengeti in search of fresh pasture. They are shadowed and preyed on by hoards of lion, cheetah, hyena and leopard. It's the attraction of this huge annual travelling larder that explains the high concentrations of lion found in the Mara. Nonetheless, at other times of the year there are still plenty of animals in the park. See **Wildlife**.

While great for animals, the reserve's rough roads ensure that visitors fully feel that they're on an expedition. Off-road driving is not officially permitted in the Mara as it destroys the delicate grassland ecosystem and, despite the thrill of the chase, you should refrain from this practise as it now threatens this remarkable environment for future generations.

   HOW TO GET THERE: From Nairobi take the A 104 north following signs for Naivasha. 65 km out of Nairobi turn left off the main road onto the B 3, signposted to Narok, which leads down, initially over rough roads, into the Rift Valley (see **A-Z**). From here it is 86 km to Narok and the road surface improves. Mount Longonot (2777 m) rises on the right of the road and Susua Volcano (2357 m) on the left. The drive to Narok takes over 2 hr. (Narok is the last place to get petrol for over 100 km.) From Narok continue on the B 3 (tarmac) for 18 km to where the road splits into three forks. The left-hand fork leads to the Loita Hills (where the Masai, see **Tribes**, remain largely undisturbed). However, continue straight on for the Masai Mara. Just a little beyond that left-hand fork the road continues straight on and you should start to see signs for Cottars, Mara Sarova and Fig Tree camps and Keekorok and Mara Sopa lodges. Enter the Mara through Sekanani Gate. From Narok to Keekorok takes about 4 hr. Nairobi approx. 260 km.

If you continue on, veering to the right, you cover some appalling roads to reach the northwest corner of the Masai Mara and the Mara River Bridge. This may take 5 hr from Narok. Kichwa Tembo tented camp is situated just outside the Oloololo Gate and this is also the entrance for Mara Serena Lodge and Governors Camp.

For those unwilling, or without the time, to make the drive there are flights twice daily from Nairobi run by Air Kenya Aviation (tel: 501421) or once a day by Executive Air Services (tel: 5006007). These fly to all the airstrips in the Masai Mara from Wilson Airport in Nairobi. The flight takes 1 hr (see **Airports**). If you book your safari through a travel agent, either at home or in Nairobi, all your travel arrangements will be organized for you.

WHERE TO STAY: *Lodges* As in all the game parks accommodation divides into three types: lodges, tented camps and public camp sites. All will organize game drives. Lodges and tented camps should be booked through travel agents.

• **Keekorok Lodge:** access via Sekanani Gate in the east of the reserve. Expensive. Swimming pool, balloon flights, tents and rooms, tarmac airstrip. (Nairobi, tel: 335807.) Where white hunters originally came to shoot lion, this is one of the oldest and best lodges in Kenya.

• **Mara Serena Lodge:** access via Oloololo Gate. Located in the centre of the reserve. Expensive. Swimming pool, all-weather airstrip, Masai dancing in the evenings. (Nairobi, tel: 338656.) Built on a hill overlooking the Mara River. The rooms are designed to resemble Masai huts. There's a hippo-watching platform down on the river.

• **Mara Sopa Lodge:** access via the Sekanani or Olaimutiek gates. Lies just outside the reserve boundary. Expensive. Swimming pool, balloon safaris. (Nairobi, tel: 20182/336088.) Has comfortable *banda* thatched huts, and offers good views over the Oloolaimutia Valley and game reserve.

WHERE TO STAY: *Camp sites* • **Governors Camp and Little Governors Camp:** access via Oloololo Gate. Located in the northwest corner of the reserve with tents on both sides of the Mara River. Expensive. Tarmac airstrip, balloon safaris. (Nairobi, tel: 331871.) Excellent accommodation, each tent having its own shower and toilet. Governors Camp looks onto the river, Little Governors onto a swamp: both attract wildlife.

• **Kichwa Tembo Camp:** at Oloololo Gate. Situated at the northwest corner, just outside the reserve. Expensive. Has its own all-weather airstrip, walking safaris, game drives and flight to Lake Victoria (see **A-Z**) to fish for Nile perch. (Nairobi, tel: 335887/335400.) Comfortable camp overlooking the reserve.

• **Mara Sarova Camp:** access via Sekanani Gate. Located in the northeast corner of the reserve. Expensive. Overlooks a water hole visited by elephant. (Nairobi, tel: 333233.) Fine views over the reserve.

• **Fig Tree Camp:** access via Talek Gate or Keekorok Lodge. Situated on the northern boundary of the reserve. Expensive. (Nairobi, tel: 21439.) Surrounded by a loop in the Talek River this pleasant camp has a relaxed but comfortable atmosphere and excellent food.

• **Cottars Camp:** situated a little before Sekanani Gate, outside the reserve. Expensive. Airstrip, walking safaris, night view of animals at a salt lick. (Nairobi, tel: 27930.) Because it stands outside the park this camp, with its natural spring, allows for night safaris and walking safaris.

Public camp sites: – there are 12 camp sites (with no facilities) along the Talek River and also outside the reserve beside the Mara River. In addition you can camp at the Musiara Gate where water is available. None of these public camp sites are all that safe (see **Camping**). There's also a camp site next to Keekorok Lodge with toilets and water. Although not terribly attractive it is safe and you can get food at the lodge canteen. You can also camp at the Mara River Camp which is just outside the reserve (park fees are collected in the camp) and in fact some of the best game can be seen on the Loita Plains and around Musiara Marsh. This camp is the only remaining one not to have an electric fence to keep the hippos out. It has a grass airstrip.

MOUNT
KENYA
SAFARI
LODGE

Nanyuki

MT KENYA
NATIONAL
PARK
Bation

NARO MORU
RIVER LODGE

Naro
Moru

A 2

ABERDARE
NATIONAL
PARK

Nyeri

A 2

A 2

Thika

A 2

Nairobi

Mt Kenya Nat. Park

Mount Kenya (see **A-Z**), at 5200 m, is the highest mountain in Kenya and the second-highest (after Kilimanjaro, see **A-Z**) on the African continent. In the early morning and those rare days when the clouds don't crowd in, its snow-capped peaks can be seen from Nyeri (see **A-Z**), Naro Moru and Nanyuki (see **A-Z**). The national park (770 sq. km) begins far down on the mountain's lower slopes. Within its boundaries are animals ranging from elephant, rhino and buffalo to leopards, monkeys and antelope (see **Wildlife**), together with unique, strangely-formed vegetation including lobelias growing to 3 m tall and giant groundsel to 6 m. During the day, Mount Kenya's positioning on the equator means temperatures can get very hot while at night the altitude ensures that they plummet.

If you have the time, and the proper camping equipment to stay out overnight, it's an experience not to miss. For an overnight stay you will need warm clothing, and if you're being ambitious and planning an ascent, a guide is definitely recommended (they can be hired in Naro Moru or Nanyuki). Mount Kenya itself has three peaks: Bation (5200 m) and Nelion (5188 m), which should only be tackled by experienced climbers, and Pt. Lenana (4900 m), which can be managed if you are fit and have a guide.

HOW TO GET THERE: Take the A 2 out of Nairobi through Thika and continue beyond the Nyeri turn-off. There's a park entrance just off the A 2 at Naro Moru from where you can drive 26 km to the weather station where the road ends. Nairobi approx. 150 km. (There are two other entrances beyond Nanyuki, however, the Naro Moru route is the most accessible.) You are advised to buy a park map in Nairobi before you leave.

WHERE TO STAY: • **Mount Kenya Safari Lodge:** on the right just before Nanyuki as you come from the south. Expensive. Swimming pool, golf course. (Nairobi, tel: 723776.) With it's fabulous views of Mount Kenya this is one of the best hotels in the country.

• **Naro Moru River Lodge:** turn right in Naro Moru and it's on the road up to the park. Moderate. (Nairobi, tel: 337501.) Provides simple accommodation. You can hire guides and equipment here for walking in the park.

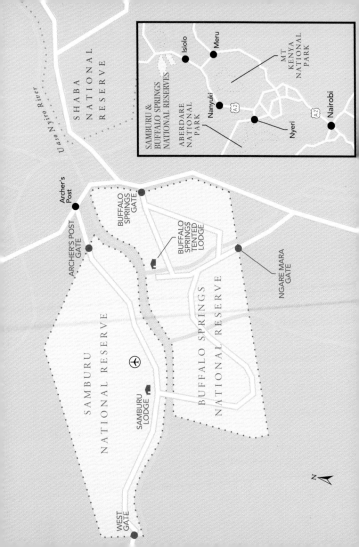

Samburu Reserve

Samburu Reserve (225 sq. km) lies to the north of Mount Kenya (see **A-Z**) and Nanyuki (see **A-Z**) in the hot low plains that stretch up to Lake Turkana (see **NAIROBI–EXCURSION 5**, **A-Z**). This reserve is one of three grouped together in this part of the country. The other two are Buffalo Springs (339 sq. km) and Shaba (239sq. km). The Samburu and Buffalo Springs reserves are separated by the Uaso Nyiro River which can be crossed by bridge. George and Joy Adamson (see **A-Z**) were instrumental in setting up these reserves. Buffalo Springs is also covered below. Most of the common game can be found in the park together with the rarer reticulated giraffe, Somalian ostrich and Grevy's zebra (larger and more finely striped than the common zebra). As ever the rivers and water holes are the most reliable locations for animal spotting. At the Samburu Lodge you may see leopard drawn to the floodlit baits laid each night. See **Wildlife**.

The actual Buffalo Springs have been encased in concrete to allow swimming (safe from crocodiles), which is more than welcome after a hard day's safari. Whether the springs are clear of bilharzia (see **Health**) is open to debate.

HOW TO GET THERE: Follow the A 2 from Nairobi to Nanyuki and onto Isiolo. Continue on a dirt track for another 18 km to reach the Ngare Mara Gate at the southern end of the reserve. Nairobi approx. 287 km. The Turkana Bus also safaris through Samburu on its trip to the lake. Tour operators organize flights to the lodges.

WHERE TO STAY: *Lodges* • **Samburu Lodge:** in the west of the reserve. Expensive. Swimming pool and airstrip. (Nairobi, tel: 335607.) Overlooking a river, meat is put out in the evenings to draw crocodiles onto the bank. There is also a floodlit area for viewing leopard.

• **Buffalo Springs Tented Lodge:** in the northeast of the Buffalo Springs Reserve. Moderate. Swimming pool. (Nairobi, tel: 336858.) Has tented accommodation and a game viewing area.

WHERE TO STAY: *Camp sites* There are camp sites just outside the reserve at the Ngare Mara Gate and also at the Buffalo Springs Gate. Security can be a problem and there have been incidents in which tourists were attacked and robbed.

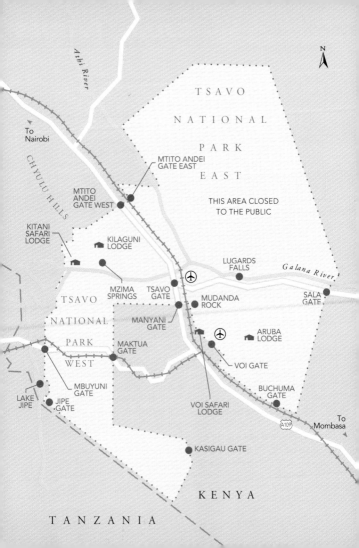

Tsavo National Park

Tsavo is Kenya's largest national park (20,800 sq. km), renowned particularly for its huge herds of elephant, which, although depleted by drought and poaching in the 1970s and 80s, are still impressive. The Nairobi–Mombasa road splits the park into two sections, Tsavo East and West, which are administered separately. All the main wildlife species are found in the park, though often the long grass makes them difficult to spot. As in the other parks, the best viewing is often to be had around water holes. See **Wildlife**.

Tsavo's lion are notorious for their ferocity, and during the development of the Nairobi–Mombasa railway (see **NAIROBI–WHAT TO SEE**) in the early 20thC a group of lions plagued the construction work, killing and eating a considerable number of the workers . Perhaps what makes the park so special, however, is its sheer size, harking back to the landscapes that greeted early explorers to Kenya.

Tsavo West

Tsavo West is notable for two particular features: Mzima Springs (see **A-Z**) and the Chyulu Hills. Mzima Springs consists of two clear-water pools inhabited by hippo and crocodile. There is an underwater viewing chamber which may afford sightings of these magnificent animals if you are lucky. Northwest of the springs stretch the Chyulu Hills and the Shetani (from the Swahili word for devil) lava flow, which erupted 200 years ago and formed a weird landscape of black solidified lava and caves. Both are well worth a visit. Lake Jipe in the south of the park is also a good place for spotting hippo.

Tsavo East

Tsavo East is not on the usual tourist trail and if you have your own transport it can be a wonderful escape into deserted savanna wilderness. The northern two-thirds of the park are closed to the public as a result of the increasingly violent poaching war being waged between wardens and poachers in search of elephant tusk and rhino horn. Take the time to visit Mudanda Rock looking out across the park over a water hole which attracts large herds of elephant in the dry season. At Lugards Falls you can expect to see crocodile. Only if you are extremely lucky will you see the black rhino which have been so severely decimated by the poachers.

HOW TO GET THERE: Gates into both Tsavo East and West are situated on the A 109 Nairobi–Mombasa road. Nairobi approx. 240 km. You can also reach Tsavo West from Amboseli on the C 103. There are no regular flights to Tsavo but aircraft can be chartered or you can fly with organized tours bookable either in Nairobi or Mombasa.

WHERE TO STAY *Tsavo West* • **Kilaguni Lodge:** near Mzima Springs and Shetani. Expensive. Swimming pool, airstrip and organized game drives. (Nairobi, tel: 336858.) A long terrace overlooks a water hole where you can see wildlife including many species of bird. There are also fine views into the Chyulu Hills and across to Mount Kilimanjaro (see **A-Z**).

• **Kitani Safari Lodge:** just south of Kilaguni Lodge. Moderate. (Nairobi, tel: 742926.) Six self-catering huts with their own bathrooms and kitchens. There is a shop for non-perishable foods, but be sure to bring your own supplies.

WHERE TO STAY: *Tsavo East* • **Voi Safari Lodge:** near Voi Gate, just off the road. Expensive. Swimming pool. (Nairobi, tel: 336858.) The lodge looks out over three water holes and across the plains from its vantage point on Woressa Hill.

• **Aruba Lodge:** access via Voi Gate. Moderate. (Nairobi, tel: 742926.) Self-catering huts with kitchen and bathroom facilities. There is a shop for basic provisions. Overlooks a water hole.

Kilaguni Lodge

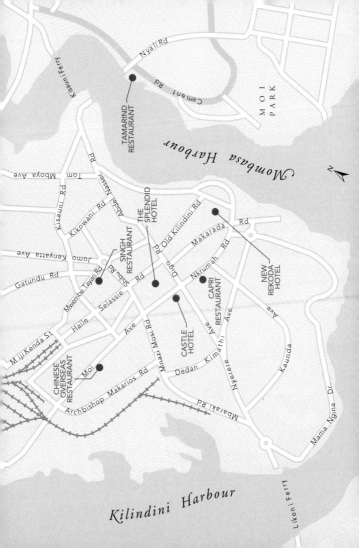

Restaurants

TAMARIND RESTAURANT Silo Rd, Nyali. Across Nyali Bridge
and on the right (15-min drive).
❑ Expensive. Reservations recommended, tel: 472263.
Looks across the creek to the Old Town (see **MOMBASA–WHAT TO SEE***),
the best view in Mombasa! Excellent food; try the seafood platter.
Dinners can also be organized aboard a cruising dhow.*

CAPRI RESTAURANT Ambalal House, Nkrumah Rd.
❑ Expensive.
Housed in a tower block but it offers some of the best food in town.

CHINESE OVERSEAS RESTAURANT Corner of Kilindini Rd
and Moi Ave.
❑ Moderate.
Serves good Chinese food in a friendly atmosphere.

SINGH RESTAURANT Mwembe Tayari Rd.
❑ Inexpensive.
Don't be put off by the loud décor – the curries here are delicious.

NEW REKODA HOTEL Nyeri St, Old Town.
❑ Evenings only. ❑ Inexpensive.
*Deservedly popular with locals and travellers alike for its delicious
Swahili cooking (see* **Food***); try the* maharagway *(beans cooked in
coconut milk). Eat and enjoy watching the Old Town bustle about you.*

CASTLE HOTEL Moi Ave.
❑ Inexpensive.
*Not strictly a restaurant but Mombasa's equivalent to Nairobi's Thorn
Tree Café (see* **NAIROBI–RESTAURANTS***), with its patio acting as both meet-
ing place and an ideal spot for people watching. The food is adequate.*

THE SPLENDID HOTEL Msanifu Kombo St.
❑ Inexpensive.
*It's the rooftop bar and restaurant which make this a favourite, though
the food is reasonable too.*

Nyali Rd

Cement Rd

MOI PARK

MACKINNON MARKET

Mombasa Harbour

GOVERNMENT SQUARE

N

Tom Mboya Ave

Abdel Nasser Rd

Kisauni Ferry

Kisauni Rd

Kikowani Rd

BIASHARA STREET

Jomo Kenyatta Ave

Old Kilindini Rd

Rd

Makarada Rd

OLD PORT TOURIST SHOP

Gatundu Rd

MWERIBE TAYARI

Mwembe Tayari Rd

Haile Selassie Ave

Digo Rd

MOI AVENUE

Nkrumah Ave

Nyerere Ave

Dedan Kimathi Ave

Kaunda Ave

Mji Kenda St

Moi Ave

Mnazi Mosi Rd

Archbishop Makarios Rd

Mbaraki Rd

Mama Ngina Dr

Likoni Ferry

Kilindini Harbour

There are tourist stalls selling fabrics, carvings, woven baskets, etc. all round the Moi Ave intersection with Digo Rd. Quality varies and be prepared to bargain. See **Best Buys, Opening Times**.

BIASHARA STREET
This is certainly the cloth and fabric centre of the coast, if not of Kenya. Kangas and kikois can be found in almost every imaginable design and colour along with cotton cloth and silk. Also see the kopias (Muslim caps).

GOVERNMENT SQUARE
In the Old Town, close to Fort Jesus.
The shops off the square sell almost anything but particularly carvings, carpets, Arab chests, perfumes and brasswork.

OLD PORT TOURIST SHOP
Government Sq.
Despite its name this shop is definitely worth a visit, if only for its Ethiopian silver and batiks.

MACKINNON MARKET
Off Biashara St and Digo Rd.
This is Mombasa's municipal market selling fruit and vegetables (try both the jak fruit and custard apples). There are also stores dealing in tea, coffee and spices.

MWERIBE TAYARI
Off Jomo Kenyatta Ave.
This street market bustles with life. On sale here are kikois, kangas, patterned shirts and almost anything else you care to think of.

MOI AVENUE
This street most of the up-market shops and boutiques plus some car-rental firms, travel agents and even a good bookshop, the Bahari Book Centre. For jewellery or attractive ornaments try Teadins or Kenrocks; both shops deal in gemstones.

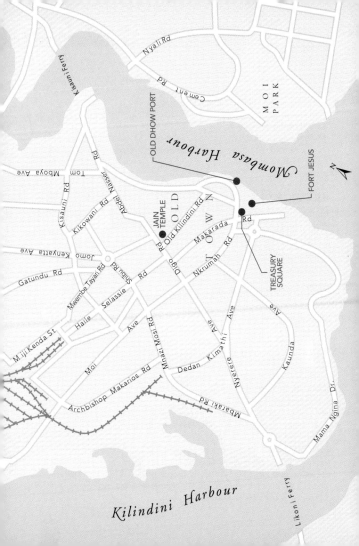

What to See

THE OLD TOWN
On the eastern side of the island.
*Mainly dating from the 19thC this maze of streets and alleyways over-
flows with a heady mixture of Arabian, African and Asian influences.
Coffee and curio shops abound. See the steps down the cliff near
Government Sq. which lead to a cave and well where slave ships used
to take on water. People will offer to guide you round the Old Town's
sights, a bargain if you get a good tour for the Kshs 4 it costs.*

FORT JESUS
Near the Old Town. ❏ 0830-1800.
*Built for the Portuguese in 1593, it served them as a bastion against
invaders and, later, it also served the forces of the Sultan of Muscat who
captured it in 1698. The cannons still look out over the entrance to the
harbour. There is also a museum with displays of coastal and traders'
artefacts up to 1000 years old. See* **A-Z**.

TREASURY SQUARE
Behind Fort Jesus.
*This square of late-19thC and early-20thC English buildings gives the
visitor a taste of Mombasa's early colonial atmosphere.*

OLD DHOW PORT
On the shore just to the north of Fort Jesus.
*A shadow of it's former self when hundreds of dhows would be moored
here loading and unloading the goods traded up the coast and across to
Arabia. A few dhows still ply the routes to Oman, Dubai, Zanzibar and
Lamu. You are no longer allowed to board the dhows but the police nor-
mally allow visitors to watch. Note: taking photographs is prohibited.*

JAIN TEMPLE
On Langoni Rd just before Digo Rd.
*Although only built in 1963, this intricate and beautiful temple is worth
seeing. The interior is perfumed and wonderfully decorated with finely-
painted ceilings and figures of deities. Jainism is a Hindu religion similar
in many respects to Buddhism.*

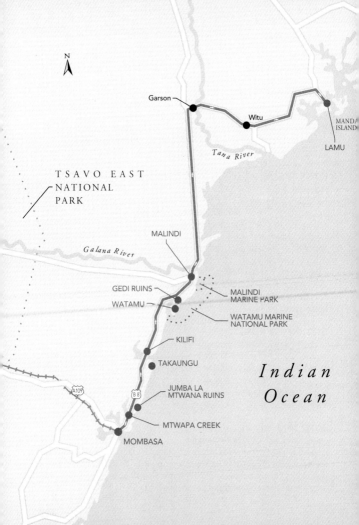

Excursion 1 North

240 km round trip. A two-day excursion north to Malindi.

Leave Mombasa across the Nyali Bridge, built in the 1970s to replace the old pontoon bridge which crossed to where the Tamarind Restaurant (see **MOMBASA–RESTAURANTS**) now stands. The toll is Kshs 5 for a car. The road north follows the coast just inland and there are more than enough beach hotels, white sands and turquoise seas to satisfy the most avid sun and sand lover.

6 km – Nyali Beach. This is Mombasa's most exclusive suburb, with well-guarded houses fronting the beach. However, access can be gained to Nyali Beach itself through the various hotel complexes and, a little further along, to Bamburi (12 km), Jomo Kenyatta (16 km) (where the past president had his beach house and where he died in 1978 – see **Kenyatta**) and Shanzu (18 km) beaches. On the left at Bamburi is Bamburi Fort. Once an old coral quarry, this has slowly been reclaimed and made into a conservation area. There is now a nature trail, crocodile and fish farms, a variety of wildlife (including buffalo, serval cats and eland) and an animal orphanage, featuring 'Sally the Hippo'. Sally was donated to the farm by wildlife cameraman Alan Root (who had adopted her when she was orphaned), after he'd captured her early years on film for a television documentary.

19 km – Mtwapa Creek. This is the site of Kenya Marineland, tel: 11-485248. It houses over 150 specimens of tropical fish, plus shark and baracuda. There is also a snake park nearby. Boats can be rented at the complex.

21 km – Jumba La Mtwana Ruins (see **A-Z**). Turn off to the right to visit these ruins and follow the track for 3 km. This 14thC Swahili village is set right on the shore. It's beginnings and desertion in the 15thC remain a mystery, though its translated name – The Slave Master's House – may give some indication of its past. See the remains of medieval African houses and two mosques, paying particular attention to the mosque by the sea. Jumba La Mtwana is also an excellent site for bird-watching (see **A-Z**). Guided tours are available. Leaving Jumba, rejoin the main road and continue north through extensive sisal estates.

46 km – Takaungu. Turn off down to the coast to this delightful white-washed Swahili village. There is a break in the reef which stretches up

the Kenya coastline and the waters of this creek are deep, clear and blue. The sealife is fascinating and snorkelling in this little-visited spot will be well rewarded. There is no accommodation at Takaungu. Rejoin the main road.

56 km – Kilifi. Noted for the ferry which, until recently, was used to carry vehicles across the creek to connect with the road north to Malindi. A new bridge (which was due to be finished by March 1991) will bring an end to this slow but pleasant respite from the journey. Long popular with Kenya's European residents Kilifi has, to date, been largely bypassed by the tourist industry. On the south shore is the village of Mnarani and the Mnarani Club Hotel which offers accommodation, welcome refreshments and fine views up and down the creek. North of Kilifi it is difficult to gain access to the beaches. Continue north to Malindi.

101 km – Turn off to Watamu and 1 km down the road you'll find Gedi National Park. Sited here are the best-preserved ruins of a Swahili town on the whole coast (see **Gedi**). In fact the ruins (covering 18 ha) are set inland, though when it was built in the 13thC the town stood on a river which has since changed its course. Surrounded by jungle, Gedi can be an eery place with its Great Mosque Palace and large, silent houses.

Keep your eyes skinned for colobus monkeys (see **Wildlife**) and a wide variety of birdlife. There is also a small museum displaying artefacts recovered from the site (0700-1800; Kshs 80).

Continue a further 44 km down the track to Watamu Marine National Park. A resort complex has been built up around the marine park (see **National Parks & Reserves**) and some of the best snorkelling on the coast is to be found at Watamu. Gorgeous coral gardens and an astonishing array of fish make either swimming or viewing from glass-bottomed boats an experience not to be missed. Trips can be arranged from most hotels in Malindi or from Watamu itself. (Park admission Kshs 80.) Rejoin the main road and continue north.

117 km – Malindi (see **A-Z**). A laid-back resort town, buzzing with European tourists in high season and delightfully quiet in low. Arabs occupied the town from the 13thC (see **Arab Influence**) and it was visited by the Portuguese explorer Vasco da Gama in 1498. There are several mosques (you'll hear the muezzin morning and evening as his call to prayer reverberates over loudspeakers throughout the town) and a large market which lives off the tourist trade. There are also plenty of hotels and restaurants ranging from expensive to very cheap. A break in the reef at Malindi which allows breakers to curl onto the beach makes it popular with the surfing fraternity.

Malindi Marine Park, lying to the south of the town, has excellent coral reefs. Glass-bottomed boats can be hired, though obviously these are cheaper if taken by a group. Most hotels arrange trips, though you'll find yourself beating off the touts trying to persuade you to book your trip via them.

Tsavo East (see **GAME PARKS–TSAVO**) is approx. 100 km away and can be reached by car from Malindi. However, check first as this section of the national park is periodically closed as a result of the war which rages between elephant and rhino poachers and the authorities.

From Malindi you can return to Mombasa or continue north to Lamu – 220 km away (see **MOMBASA–EXCURSION 2**).

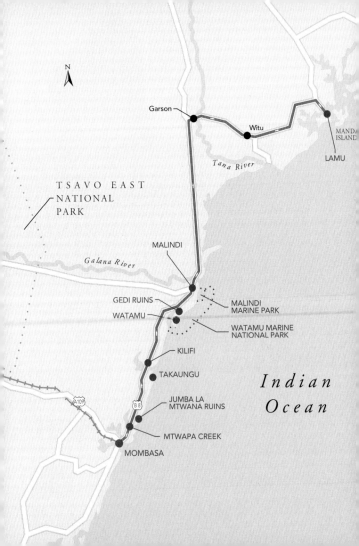

Excursion 2 Lamu

440 km round trip. A two-day excursion to a fascinating Muslim town.

The bus to Lamu (see **A-Z**) leaves Malindi (see **A-Z**) at 1100 (using the
Tana River or Coast bus companies). You should book a ticket beforehand to ensure you get a seat. The 220 km journey north to Lamu over
dirt-track roads is hot and rigorous. It takes over 6 hr, with brief stops at
Garson on the Tana River and at Witu. Alternatively, it is possible to fly
to Lamu from Malindi, Mombasa or Nairobi with Kenya Aviation Ltd.
There are four flights daily from Mombasa via Malindi, and one daily
from Nairobi costing Kshs 2000. Planes land at Manda Island and you
then cross to Lamu itself by boat.

This traditional Swahili town has long been a world apart. No cars are
allowed on the island (apart from the District Commissioner's), but
instead heavily-laden donkeys career down Lamu's narrow white-
washed streets and alleyways. Dhows bob in the harbour, some still
continuing the ancient trade with Oman. Lamu was founded over 1000
years ago and was an important base for the slave trade with the Arab
world. In the 19thC it became an Omani protectorate. The combination
of the onset of the British Empire, which made Mombasa the principal
coastal port, and the abolition of slavery, reduced Lamu to a sleepy
backwater, an atmosphere which did much to attract the first travellers

to its quiet streets in the 1960s. Now fishing and tourism are it's major industries. That said, the numerous mosques and particularly the annual feast of Maulidi (to celebrate Mohammed's birth) which draws thousands of Muslim pilgrims, ensure the retention of Lamu's strong Islamic identity (see **Arab Influence**).

There are two smart hotels on the island: Petley's, in the town, and Peponi's, at the near end of the extensive beach. There are also plenty of cheap lodgings to be found in the town, particularly the New Mahrus Hotel and the Lamu Guest House. There are good restaurants both at Peponi's and Petley's and countless others serving mainly Indian and Swahili food (see **A-Z**). Don't walk past the Yoghurt Inn – its popularity is well-deserved.

Lamu town is fascinating to wander round, with a maze of alleyways, mosques and ancient houses, so set aside at least one day of your stay to enjoy its unique atmosphere. On the waterfront, next to Petley's, you'll find the Museum (0830-1230, 1430-1700) displaying exhibits of the town's Swahili and Arabic past. The post office, bank, airline office and old town gate are also to be found here, though it can be pleasant just to sit on the harbour edge, watching the dhows and Muslim women in their black buibuis (shawls).

In the town itself the fort, which was once an Omani Palace, is now a prison. Most of the mosques have huge, open doorways allowing visitors to see in from the street; men, if well covered, will be allowed to enter, though unfortunately women are not. The Riyadha Mosque is particularly ornate and the centre of the Maulidi Feast which is held in late Sep./early Oct. There are also numerous craft shops in the town.

A 45 min walk from the town leads to Shela and Lamu beaches. Peponi's is situated at the top end, nearest the town, and beyond it stretch 12 km of crescent beach washed by curling breakers from the open sea. It's not difficult to find a patch to yourself. You can hire a dhow to take you round to the beach from the town. Dhow trips out to the other islands of Manda and Pate can be arranged in town. Prices vary depending on where you go but do negotiate. Trips usually involve fishing en route and barbecuing your catch on deserted sands. Idyllic!

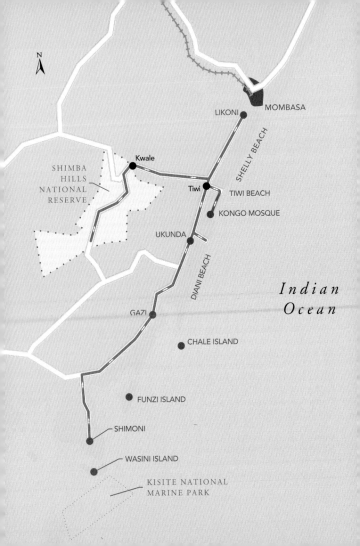

N

MOMBASA

LIKONI

SHELLY BEACH

Kwale

SHIMBA
HILLS
NATIONAL
RESERVE

Tiwi

TIWI BEACH

KONGO MOSQUE

UKUNDA

DIANI BEACH

*Indian
Ocean*

GAZI

CHALE ISLAND

FUNZI ISLAND

SHIMONI

WASINI ISLAND

KISITE NATIONAL
MARINE PARK

156 km round trip. A one- or two-day excursion south along the coast to Shimoni.

Leave Mombasa for the south coast using the busy Likoni ferry. The crossing takes about seven minutes though you may have a much longer wait to get on it. A bridge has been proposed but has yet to materialize. However, this does mean that, apart from the resort area of Diani, the south coast is less developed than the north. There is not much at Likoni although the Shelly Beach Hotel (5 km off to the left) provides reasonable accommodation and access to a good coral reef. There is also a camp site at Shelley Beach. However, swimming is only feasible at high tide. Continue south, heading for Tiwi Beach.

18 km – Shimba Hills National Reserve. Turn off to the right following signposts for Kwale. 17 km up this road and beyond the town of Kwale is the main gate for the Shimba Hills National Reserve. At over 400 m the reserve provides a welcome break from the heat and humidity of the coastal strip, as well as a chance for beach holiday-makers to catch a glimpse of Kenya's famed wildlife. The reserve itself is small (just under 2000 sq. km) and relatively little visited. Elephant, buffalo and giraffe can be seen as well as the rare sable and roan antelope. Only the extremely fortunate will spot the few lion and leopard in the park (see **Wildlife**). However, the views down to the coast from this haven are delightful. There is one game lodge, the Shimba Hills Lodge (expensive), built in the trees. A camp site, with huts for rent, is sited 3 km from the main gate. The best wildlife viewing is in the early morning or late evening. Return to the coast road and continue south.

23 km – Tiwi. Turn left off the main road and follow the track for 3 km to the seashore. Tiwi has an attractive beach with plenty of moderately-priced accommodation in the form of beach cottages. (Of particular note are Sand Island beach cottages and Twiga Lodge.) The south end of Tiwi Beach is bounded by the Tiwi River which can be forded in the dry season to visit the Kongo Mosque, at the north end of Diani Beach. This ruined, rather eerie mosque, still used to celebrate Islamic holy days, is surrounded by thick-trunked baobab trees. It should be noted that it can be dangerous to walk alone away from the hotels around Tiwi. Rejoin the main road and continue south.

28 km – Ukunda. This village is situated at the turn-off to the coastal strip of Diani Beach. As the best stretch of beach in the south, Diani has attracted the attention of tour operators and accordingly there are numerous hotels along its 5 km stretch. However, all are well-spaced and there is none of the cramped package-tour feel common in the Mediterranean. The beach itself is a wide, gently-sloping expanse of fine white sand. The sea is clear and brilliant blue, hemmed in by a coral reef which is an easy swim away. The reef, with its attendant aquatic life, also ensures no unwelcome predatory species can reach the inner lagoon. There are facilities for windsurfing, water-skiing, parascending and snorkelling, both at the hotels and from huts on the beach. Big game fishing can also be arranged at most hotels, though the main operator is John Bland (Diani, tel: 2087). Restaurants abound in all the hotel complexes but particularly noteworthy are the Nomad's Restaurant and Ali Barbour's, the latter set in a natural coral cave with an excellent French menu. Nightlife revolves almost exclusively round the large hotels with discos, bars and occasional live music. However, for most people evenings consist of soothing the sunburn, dinner, and moonlit strolls on the beach.

Ukunda serves as Diani's village and has a bank (1000-1300 Mon.-Fri.), shopping centre and post office (0800-1230, 1400-1700 Mon.-Fri.). Rejoining the main road and continuing south the coastal resorts peter out. However, there are attractive beaches at Gazi, offshore at Chale Island which can be reached by boat, and Funzi Island which can be walked to at low tide. There is little in the way of accommodation and you'll need your own transport to reach them.

78 km – Shimoni. The village has long been a mecca for game fishing enthusiasts. There are two lodges which cater specifically for them: the Pemba Channel Fishing Club and the Shimoni Reef Fishing Lodge. Scuba diving and snorkelling with instruction can also be arranged. Wasini Island lies just offshore, surrounded by crystal-clear waters and coral beds. Boats can be arranged from Shimoni. Boat trips can also be arranged down to Kisite National Marine Park, either from the restaurant in the village on Wasini island or from Shimoni. Along the coral reefs you'll find the best snorkelling in Kenya. Return to Mombasa on the coast road.

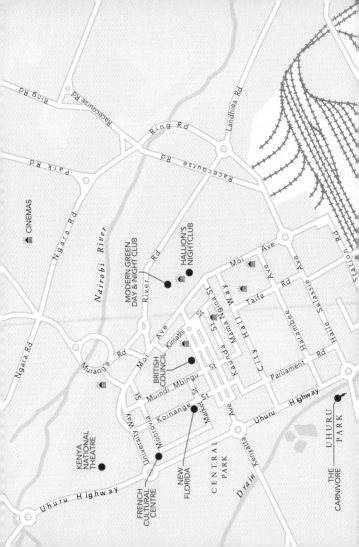

Nightlife

See **Nightlife**, **Opening Times**.

THE CARNIVORE Langata Rd, just beyond Wilson Airport.
❏ Expensive.
There is a disco on Sat. night and sometimes live bands on Wed. and Fri. Frequented by Nairobi's young and wealthy (known as Wabenzis due to their predilection for Mercedes Benz cars).

NEW FLORIDA Koinange St, near the City Market.
❏ Moderate.
*Resembling a striped orange mushroom, it's hard to miss! Good music system. Like it or not, if you're not accompanied, you'll soon be approached in this atmospheric club. Single men beware (see **Health**).*

MODERN GREEN DAY & NIGHT CLUB Latema Rd, off River Rd and near the Iqbal Hotel.
❏ Free.
That the bar is caged off from the clientele says a lot about the club. Go to watch and watch yourself. Only for the adventurous, but a lot of fun all the same.

HALLION'S NIGHTCLUB Tom Mboya St, parallel to Moi Ave.
❏ Inexpensive.
Good, fun club, which is popular with travellers. Cold beer and a relaxed atmosphere. There's a live band most evenings.

CINEMA
There are several in the city centre area showing a selection of English and American movies. For the uninitiated and mobile, the drive-in on the Thika road is an interesting alternative.

THEATRE, CONCERTS & LECTURES
The Professional Centre (on Parliament Rd) and the Kenya National Theatre (opposite the Norfolk Hotel) provide a range of drama. The latter has classical concerts about once a month. The British Council and French Cultural Centre also organize concerts and lectures.

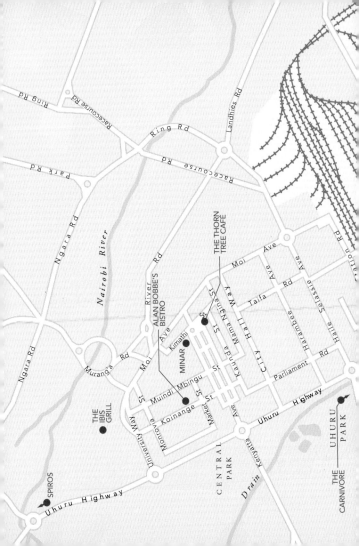

Restaurants

See **Eating Out, Opening Times**.

THE IBIS GRILL Norfolk Hotel, at the top of Harry Thuku Rd.
❏ Evenings. Reservations and jacket required.
❏ Expensive.
The hotel has a place in Nairobi's colonial heritage while the Grill serves wonderful cuisine. Before your meal go for a drink in Lord Delamere's Bar where Kenya's young whites hang out.

ALAN BOBBE'S BISTRO Koinange St, in the Cartex Building.
❏ Lunch & evenings. ❏ Expensive.
Small but delightful. The food is delicious, especially the seafood dishes. During the filming of Out of Africa *this was one of Robert Redford's favourite Nairobi restaurants.*

THE CARNIVORE Langata Rd, beyond Wilson Airport. A 33 km drive from the city centre.
❏ Evenings. Reservations recommended, tel: 501775. ❏ Expensive.
Great restaurant which, as the name suggests, specializes in barbecued meat including wildebeest, zebra and giraffe, as well as more usual fare.

THE THORN TREE CAFÉ New Stanley Hotel, Kimathi St.
❏ Breakfast, lunch & evenings. ❏ Moderate.
Perhaps Nairobi's best-known café and meeting place. It is outdoors and has an acacia tree growing up through it's centre which travellers use as a notice board. Central and relaxed, though the service is slow.

SPIROS 2nd floor, Westlands Mall, 5 min from the city centre.
❏ Lunch & evenings. ❏ Moderate.
Greek restaurant with excellent food and pleasant, informal surroundings. A new favourite with the mzungu (whites) and expat communities.

MINAR Banda St, near the intersection with Kimathi St.
❏ Lunch & evenings. ❏ Inexpensive.
Of Nairobi's many Indian restaurants this is probably the best value for money. It may look somewhat jaded but the food is delicious.

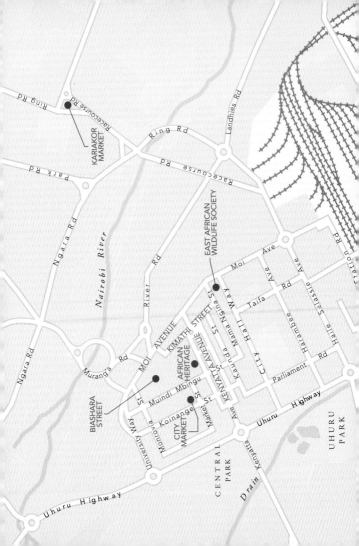

KARIAKOR MARKET

Ring Rd

Racecourse Rd

Ring Rd

Landhies Rd

Park Rd

Racecourse Rd

Ngara Rd

Ngara Rd

Nairobi River

River Rd

EAST AFRICAN WILDLIFE SOCIETY

Mol Ave

Ngara Rd

Muranga Rd

MOI AVENUE

KIMATHI STREET

Tom Mboya St

Taifa Rd

City Hall Rd

Kaunda St

Mama Ngina St

Station Rd

Haile Selassie Ave

Harambee Ave

Muindi Mbingu St

AFRICAN HERITAGE

KENYATTA AVENUE

BIASHARA STREET

University Way

Monrovia St

Koinange St

Market St

CITY MARKET

Parliament Rd

Uhuru Highway

Uhuru Highway

CENTRAL PARK

Kenyatta Ave

Drain

UHURU PARK

Shopping

CITY MARKET Between Koinange St and Muindi Mbingu St.
Undoubtedly the tourist market in central Nairobi. You'll find jewellery, baskets, wood and soapstone carvings and batiks. You'll get the hard sell so bargain hard. The covered building houses the fruit and vegetable section which is definitely worth a visit. See **Markets**.

KARIAKOR MARKET On the Ring Rd.
Take bus 7, 8 or 9 from the Hilton Hotel, a matatu (see **A-Z**) *or taxi. A great many of the goods that you buy in town are made out here. In the enclosed market baskets are woven, carvings completed and '1000 mile' shoes constructed from old tyres. There are literally hundreds of baskets of sisal, wool and plastic (see* **Best Buys**) *for sale both within and outside the market. If you can manage the journey this is a 'must', and far better than the City Market. See* **Markets**.

BIASHARA STREET Off Koinange St, behind the City Market.
This is Nairobi's main street for buying cloth. These shops, mostly Asian, stock a wide range of kangas and kikois. If you're looking for bags you're most likely to find what you want here as well.

AFRICAN HERITAGE Kenyatta Ave, behind the ICEA building.
Not only the biggest curio shop in Nairobi but, more importantly, probably the best. It stocks a wide selection of tribal jewellery and carvings from other parts of Africa as well as Kenya. Also see the batiks and paintings. While the quality is good the prices are high. Even if you're not buying it's certainly worth a browse.

EAST AFRICAN WILDLIFE SOCIETY Hilton Hotel, Watali St, off Mania Nginan St.
If you want good-quality drawings and prints this is a good place to come, though again it's fairly pricey.

KENYATTA AVENUE, MOI AVENUE & KIMATHI STREET
These are the main shopping streets if you need toiletries or other general items for your stay.

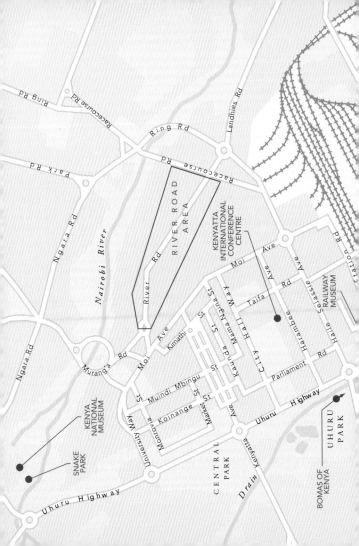

What to See

BOMAS OF KENYA On Langata Rd, past Wilson Airport at the junction with Mugadi Rd.
❑ 1430 Mon.-Fri., 1530 Sat. & Sun.
Traditional Kenyan tribal dances are performed in an amphitheatre.

KENYA NATIONAL MUSEUM Museum Hill, at the top of Uhuru Highway.
❑ 0930-1800. ❑ Kshs 30 for non-residents, Kshs 10 for residents.
The best museum in and about East Africa with excellent palaeontological and cultural displays as well as extensive exhibits of flora and fauna.

SNAKE PARK, Museum Hill, opposite the National Museum.
❑ 0930-1800. ❑ Kshs 30 for non-residents, Kshs 10 for residents.
Fascinating collection of snakes, including black mambas, pythons, puff adders and spitting cobras. Also has a crocodile pool and aquarium.

RAILWAY MUSEUM Bottom of Station Rd, next to the Uhuru Highway, a few minutes walk from the railway station.
❑ 0830-1630 Mon.-Fri., 0830-1530 Sat. ❑ Kshs 5.
Recounts the history of railways in Kenya. The museum displays exhibits from the building of the Mombasa–Uganda line which opened up Kenya to the colonial settlers in the late 19thC. The display includes the coach from which a police inspector was dragged and eaten as he lay in wait to kill one of the lions, known as the 'Man-eater of Tsavo', that plagued the early construction work.

KENYATTA INTERNATIONAL CONFERENCE CENTRE City Sq., off Harambee Ave.
*Nairobi's tallest building offers unparalleled views of the city and its surroundings. On a clear day you can see Mount Kenya and Kilimanjaro (see **A-Z**) to the south. There is a revolving restaurant at the top.*

RIVER ROAD AREA East of the centre, beyond Moi Ave.
*The heart of the city where Asian, African and Western influences merge in a melee of bustle and noise. Numerous cheap restaurants and hotels. Worth a visit but leave valuables in your hotel (see **Crime & Theft**).*

Excursion 1 National Park

A one-day trip to see wildlife in a park on the outskirts of the city.

Organized tours can easily be arranged through most travel agents in Nairobi city centre. The park is open 0600-1900; admission Kshs 80. Leave Nairobi on the Uhuru Highway to join Langata Rd and follow signs for Wilson Airport and Karen (see **Nairobi**). 10 km from the city and 3 km past the airport, turn left into the park.

Nairobi National Park is an astonishing testament to the adaptability of its animal inhabitants. Within sight of a city of over one million people lion, cheetah, giraffe, impala, wildebeest, zebra, rhino, hippo and crocodiles can all be found (see **Wildlife**). Indeed, within its 114 sq. km you are likely to have a better opportunity to spot certain animals, most notably rhino, than in almost any of the country's other national parks. Before starting the tour of the park it's worth stopping to visit the Animal Orphanage which is situated next to the main gate. The orphanage takes care of sick, stray and abandoned animals until they are well enough to be released back into the park. It's an excellent place to see leopard, cheetah and several other species that you are unlikely to come across, close up, in the wild.

Entering through the Langata Gate, drive along a ridge through forests where giraffe, rhino and possibly even leopard can be seen. From Impala Hill, standing at the end of the forested ridge, you look out over plains to the east where you can see game roaming, the clusters of Kombi vans full of tourists signposting lion and cheetah finds. In fact the game wardens keep a close check on the movements of these two predators, so if you ask at the gate you'll be directed to the most likely sites. Further out on the plains to the southeast the Mbagathi-Athi River marks the park's southern boundary and in its pools hippo and crocodiles can be seen. Out on the plains look out for ostrich and secretary birds.

The best times to visit the park, as elsewhere, are at dawn and dusk when the predators are on the move.

Note: Do not get out of your car while inside the park, except at points where signposts indicate that it is safe to do so (see **Safaris**).

Excursion 2 Karen

50 km round trip. A one-day excursion to Karen and the Ngong Hills.

Leave Nairobi on the Uhuru Highway, following Langata Rd out past Nairobi National Park (see **NAIROBI–EXCURSION 1**). Continue along Langata Rd.

16 km – Langata. Turn off onto Langata South Rd, following this through Langata itself to reach the Rothschild Giraffe Centre (1600-1730 school days, 1000-1730 weekends, 0930-1730 school holidays; Kshs 50) on Gogo Falls Rd which lies off Koitobos Rd. The centre was established by an American couple to protect the rare Rothschild giraffe. The animals themselves are tame and will even eat out of your hand. It's a great way to see these beautiful

animals close up and an excellent excursion for children. The centre is set in the grounds of an old settler's house, which provides both an evocative backdrop for giraffe viewing and a fascinating glimpse back to pre-independence days. It was used as a location in the film *White Mischief*. Return to Langata Rd and continue out towards Karen.

18 km – Karen. At the Karen Dukas Shopping Centre, situated at a crossroads, follow Karen Rd past the Country Club until you reach Karen College, which is built in the grounds of Karen Blixen's (see **A-Z**) house (0900-1800; Kshs 50). This is where the Danish author of *Out of Africa* had her coffee farm in the 1920s. The Danish Government gave the house to Kenya on the granting of independence. However, it was the filming of *Out of Africa* and the attendant publicity which encouraged the government to run the house as a museum. With its wood-panelled rooms, veranda and some original furniture, the house gives the visitor some idea of life in those heady days. Returning to the cross-roads, take Ngong Rd signposted to Ngong.

25 km – Ngong Town. From here you can either drive or walk up into the Ngong Hills. Turn right uphill when you reach the town. The track leads up to the top of one hill, which is easily identifiable by the radio pylons near the summit. The Ngong Hills form a barrier between the

plain surrounding Nairobi and the Rift Valley (see **A-Z**). They stand at 2500 m and from their peaks there are wonderful views of the surrounding countryside. The arid volcanic landscape of the Rift Valley lies to one side with Nairobi on the other while, on a clear day, if you're lucky, you might even catch sight of Mount Kenya (see **GAME PARKS**, **A-Z**) to the north. The Masai (see **Tribes**) say that the Ngong's distinctive knuckle shape was formed by the grip of a giant's hand as he stumbled on the ridge. Whatever their origins they have long been a favourite with Nairobi's residents. Today the loss of much of the forestation and subsequent fall in the numbers of animals on the hills' slopes, combined with a reputation for robberies, have made them less popular, and safe, than in the past (see **Crime & Theft**). Accordingly it is advisable to visit the Ngong's in groups or by booking through one of the many tour operators in Nairobi.

Return to Nairobi by retracing your steps.

Excursion 3 Naivasha/Nakuru

440 km round trip. A two- or three-day excursion north to Nyeri, taking in lakes Naivasha and Nakuru, Hell's Gate and Thomson's Falls.

Leave Nairobi on the A 104 following the signs for Naivasha. As you travel along the escarpment you will be afforded stunning views west across the Rift Valley (see **A-Z**) to Mount Longonot.

89 km – Naivasha. Turn off the A 104 into the town which has little to keep you, unless you need food for camping, and continue to the lake itself. Lake Naivasha (see **A-Z**) is one of the few freshwater lakes in the Rift Valley and was a Masai (see **Tribes**) centre for watering their cattle, until the Europeans arrived and commandeered the surrounding lands. However, it's the sheer natural beauty of the area plus the abundant birdlife (see **Bird-watching**) on the lake which attracts people today. There are several lodges, some with camping facilities, where you can stay. Crescent Island is worth a visit with its monkeys, gazelle, waterbuck, python and several hundred species of bird. The 'island' is in fact the rim of a submerged volcanic crater which forms a lake within a lake when Naivasha's waters are really low. The water levels in recent years have dropped, making the island accessible from the shore. Otherwise enquire at the Lake Naivasha Hotel about boat trips out.

The turn-off for Hell's Gate is about a third of the way round the rough lakeshore road. Otherwise known as the Njorowa Gorge, Hell's Gate (see **A-Z**) begins as a plain, where you can see a whole range of wildlife, which narrows into a steep-sided and very 'African'-looking gorge with towering rock pinnacles. The gorge is a volcanic feature with natural steam jets and hot springs in its depths and it's an excellent and exciting place to hike and rock-climb. Keep glancing upwards for glimpses of the eagles, buzzards and vultures that breed in the cliffs. You may be lucky and spot the rare lammergeier vulture.

Finally, at Lake Naivasha, near the Safariland Lodge, is Elsamere, where Joy and George Adamson lived. The Adamsons (see **A-Z**) are famous for their work with lions including, of course, Elsa, immortalized in the book and film *Born Free*. Members of wildlife societies may be allowed to stay overnight; other visitors are welcome from 1500-1700 daily.

Rejoin the A 104 at Naivasha. If you have a hardy vehicle and have driven round the lake, you will join the A 104 just north of the town.

Continue travelling north. Approaching Nakuru you catch sight of Lake Nakuru,

which may be ringed with a pale pink necklace of flamingos.

156 km – Nakuru (see **A-Z**). A dusty 'settlers' town, supplying surrounding farms with essential agricultural foodstuffs, seeds and fertilizers. It has banks and accommodation. Having soaked up the colonial atmosphere, unless you have a compelling reason to stay, push straight on to the wonderful Lake Nakuru National Park which lies just outside the town (entrance Kshs 80). The park was created for its population of pink lesser flamingos. In the 1960s there were some two million of them. In recent years numbers have fallen periodically as a result of changes in the lake's alkalinity, which affects the algae the flamingos feed off. At such times the flamingos usually migrate north to Lake Bogoria (see **A-Z**) (approx. 3 hr drive). If they're in residence they form one of the natural world's most spectacular sights. Even if the flamingos are not there in numbers, other animals will be. There are pelicans and hippo in the lake, while in the forests live waterbuck, impala, Rothschild giraffe, monkeys and baboons (see **Wildlife**). In the park you can stay at the Lake National Lodge, Sarova Lion Hill Hotel or at one of the camp sites, though beware of thieving baboons! Return to Nakuru and follow the B 5 and signposts to Nyahururu.

225 km – Nyahururu. A cool bustling town at almost 2500 m above sea level. Continue through the town following signposts to Nyeri. Just outside Nyahururu turn right for Thomson's Falls Lodge. Here you can see the attractive 80 m-high waterfalls, named after the explorer Joseph Thomson (see **Exploration**), which crash into a steep, richly-vegetated gorge. A walk to the bottom through forests damp with spray is a pleasant escape from the souvenir stalls that have congregated at the top. From here rejoin the road to Nyeri which skirts the north and western edge of the Aberdare (see **A-Z**) mountain range, passing through the rich arable farmland that was once the preserve of the white colonial class.

335 km – Nyeri (see **A-Z**). An attractive town with plenty of accommodation, cafés and restaurants. It is a Kikuyu (see **Tribes**) town and a centre for excursions to the Aberdares (see **GAME PARKS-ABERDARE**). Leave Nyeri and join the A 2. Either go north to Mount Kenya (see **A-Z**) or south to Thika (not as enticing as the title of the novel, *The Flame Trees of Thika* might lead you to expect) and on to Nairobi (105 km).

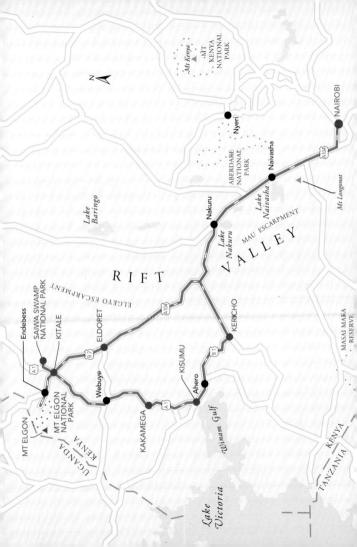

Excursion 4 Western Kenya

800 km round trip. A two- or three-day excursion west to Kericho, taking in Mount Elgon, Kisumu and Lake Victoria.

Leave Nairobi on the A 104 to Naivasha and Nakuru.

156 km – Nakuru (see **NAIROBI–EXCURSION 3**). Continue travelling northwest on the A 104 following signs for Eldoret, first crossing the Rift Valley (see **A-Z**) then climbing steeply to nearly 2700 m at the Mau Summit and on between the Nandi and Elgeyo Escarpments.

311 km – Eldoret (see **A-Z**). A pleasant farming and market town which has retained a rather old-world charm both in appearance and character. If you stop over here the New Lincoln Hotel (on Nandi Rd) can be recommended for a taste of times past. Apart from its pleasant atmosphere there is little to keep you in Eldoret so continue on the A 104, turning onto the B 2 where it's signposted to Kitale.

325 km – Kitale (see **A-Z**). An attractive town, smaller than, but similar to, Eldoret. The centre of the local farming community, it has a temperate climate, standing as it does at 1800 m. Accommodation can be found at the Kitale Club, as you enter the town, or for the more discriminating, at the private Lokitela Farm 18 km west of Kitale, tel: Nairobi 882253 or write to PO Box 122, Kitale. Kitale is an excellent place to base yourself for exploring the Saiwa Swamp and for excursions to Mount Elgon National Park.

For Saiwa Swamp, travel north on the A 1 for 18 km, turning right at the sign and following a track for 6 km to the park gates. The Saiwa Swamp National Park is only 2 sq. km in size and was created specifically for the protection of the Sitatunga, a large antelope that spends much of its time submerged to the neck in water. You can watch them, together with colobus and vervet monkeys, from the observation towers. Saiwa Swamp can only be visited on foot.

Mount Elgon National Park is reached by following signs to the village of Endebess,19 km northwest of Kitale, and then continuing for a further 10 km to enter via the Chorlim Gate. Mount Elgon (see **A-Z**) sits astride the Kenya-Uganda border and climbs from jungle, through forests to peak moorland. Elephant, buffalo, a variety of antelope, bush-pig and leopard may all be seen. However, what most people come to see are the Kitum Caves. These caves honeycomb the lower reaches of Mount Elgon near the Chorlim Gate. For years elephants have entered and enlarged the caves by digging for salt with their tusks. They come at night so bring a torch and sleeping bag. To reach the Kenyan summit of Mount Elgon, Koitobos Peak, follow the park trail to its end, from where it's about a 2.5 hr hike to the top. There are camp sites just inside the Chorlim Gate and the rather basic Mount Elgon Lodge outside. After your trip up the mountain return to Kitale. From Kitale follow the A 1 south through attractive countryside signposted to Kakamega.

432 km – Kakamega. Once a gold rush town, today it has little of interest. Continue south on the A 1.

442 km – Turn left off the A 1 at the petrol station and follow the road 13 km through Shinyahi village to the Kakamega Forest Station. Kakamega Forest (see **A-Z**) is true jungle, and was once part of the jungles that spread right across central Africa. As such it has a stupendous variety of plant life and it's also a haven for wildlife, particularly birds. Keep your eyes peeled for the great blue touraco, hornbills and the black-and-white colobus monkeys. Early morning is perhaps the best time to visit the forest though an evening excursion with a torch may be rewarded with sightings of fruit bats and flying squirrels. Beware the snakes, particularly the gaboon viper, and don't wear sandals. In fact, if you're worried about snakes, it's best to wear long trousers tucked into socks, and boots. Rejoin the A 1 and continue south to Kisumu.

474 km – Kisumu (see **A-Z**). The town stands on the shores of Lake Victoria (see **A-Z**) and is Kenya's third-largest town. Once it thrived on trade with Uganda and Tanzania but recent years have seen something of a decline (though improving conditions across the border look likely to reverse this trend). Nonetheless it's a delightful town with a relaxed atmosphere dictated by the heat and high humidity. Boat trips on to the lake or ferries to other Kenyan towns around the Winam Gulf can be organized. The Sunset Hotel overlooking the lake on the south of the town is worth a visit, either to spend the night or just to watch the sun-

set over dinner. If you don't have your own transport the railway connecting Kisumu to Nairobi is a good option. Follow the B 1 southeast through Ahero as the road climbs steadily to Kericho.

553 km – Kericho (see **A-Z**). Outside Sri Lanka and India, Kenya is the world's largest tea-growing country and Kericho sits in the heartland (see **Tea**). With most of the workers living out on the estates the town itself is geared very much to supplying them. You can stay in the unsurprisingly named Tea Hotel which may be able to organize a visit to one of the estates. Surrounding the town are rolling hills swathed in the green of growing tea, fed with a regular diet of morning sunshine and afternoon showers. Continue on the B 1 eastwards, following signs for Nakuru.

560 km – Turn right off the B 1 to the Kericho Arboretum. These delightful gardens, comprising trees from all over the world, lead down to a small lake. The Mau Forest begins where the arboretum ends, thick mountain vegetation reaching up to the Mau Escarpment. Even at its edge there are hoards of fabulously coloured butterflies and the constant call of the birdlife. This is an excellent spot to pause for a picnic. Rejoin the B 1 and climb over the Mau Escarpment to the Mau Summit. Join the A 104 returning to Nakuru and Nairobi (266 km).

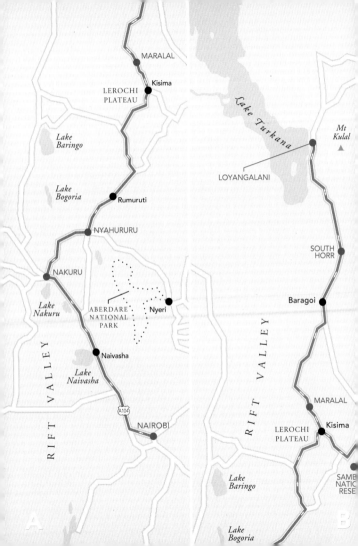

Excursion 5 Lake Turkana

1000 km round trip. An arduous but fascinating excursion, taking several days, into the plains and deserts of northern Kenya and onto Loyangalani and Lake Turkana.

The journey north to Lake Turkana (see **A-Z**) takes the traveller through what was once the evocatively-named Northern Frontier District. While many more visitors now make this trip than previously it still takes you into the harsh desert hinterland bordering Sudan and Ethiopia and accordingly should not be undertaken lightheartedly. There are essentially three methods of making the journey:

Overland Truck: Travelling in a Bedford or Mercedes truck with around 20 other passengers can take anywhere between 7-10 days to make the round trip. Camping en route, with a driver and cook, they mostly head for Loyangalani from Nairobi with stops at Samburu (see **GAME PARKS-SAMBURU**) or Lake Baringo (see **A-Z**) , Maralal and South Horr. They are the most popular means of visiting the lake and comparatively cheap – although in high season you may need to book several weeks in advance. The main operators are:

Safari Camp Services, Koinange St, Nairobi, tel: 330130. The original 'Turkana Bus' departs every 2nd Sat. and takes a week via Maralal, South Horr, Loyangalani and Samburu.

Game Trackers, Nairobi, tel: 338927. Via Lake Baringo, Loyangalani and Samburu. Departs Fri. in high season, every 2nd Fri. in low season, and takes eight days.

Special Camping Safaris, Nairobi, tel: 338325. Via Lake Baringo, Loyangalani, Samburu and Mount Kenya (see **A-Z**). Departs every 2nd Sun. and takes ten days.

Plane: Flights are best booked through tour operators who will also book your accommodation at the lodge in Loyangalani. Flights depart from Wilson Airport and take about 2 hr. Charter aircraft (see **A-Z**) can also be hired to make the trip though this is rather more expensive.

Car (do-it-yourself): You will undoubtedly require four-wheel drive transport and this is definitely not for the inexperienced. You will need to carry all you own provisions, with extra fuel cans and water. The last reliable petrol stop is at Maralal. Advise the car-hire firm (see **Car Hire**) of your planned route. You should also note that from Mar.-June and

Oct.-Nov. rain may make the roads impassable, while for the rest of the year temperatures constantly exceed 35°C. Some mechanical knowledge would be a definite advantage. Once again: this is not for the inexperienced. See **Driving**.

Leave Nairobi on the A 104 following signs for Naivasha and Nakuru. (see NAIROBI–EXCURSION 3).

117 km – Nakuru. Turn out of town and follow signs for Nyahururu.

188 km – Nyahururu. The town is a central supply point for many farmers in the Aberdares (see **A-Z**). It is also the last major town on the road up to Turkana. At just under 2500 m enjoy the cool air and lush countryside because from here it's all downhill into the baking heat of the plains. The road north leads first to Rumuruti, a farming centre in colonial times, then on through the savanna ranchland of the Lerochi Plateau. Keep your eyes open, especially if camping, as there are still lions in this area preying on both cattle and zebra.

340 km – Maralal. The end of the line in terms of towns. Situated in a hollow beneath forested hills to the north, the town is an important centre for the Samburu (see **Tribes**). Maralal itself is full of character with its dusty streets, small shops and colourful, proud inhabitants. Jomo Kenyatta (see **A-Z**) was held in detention here in 1961 before finally being released and the bungalow has been designated a national monument. The writer Wilfred Thesiger (see **A-Z**) has a house in Maralal. This is also the last place to change money on the route north and the final reliable petrol stop. Leave Maralal and climb steeply into the Podu Forests. Elephant can occasionally be spotted through the undergrowth.

365 km – There is a quite fabulous view out over the Rift Valley (see **A-Z**) at the Lesiolo Escarpment. Hills drop away steeply into a vast bowl (the bottom of which is some 250 m below sea level) of mountains and haze. It is at its best in the very early morning but nonetheless breathtaking whenever you arrive. The road becomes progressively rougher and dustier, and temperatures increasingly higher, as you drop onto the El Barta Plains. At the tiny village of Baragoi, the road curves towards the lonely mountains that enclose South Horr.

437 km – South Horr. Hemmed in by mountains on either side, the valley is surprisingly green, with flowering trees outside the mission

buildings. The excellent Kurungu camp site has showers and is fenced in. Samburu ply their wares and may agree, for a negotiated fee, to dance for you. It may be manufactured but the sight of the young *moran* working themselves into a jumping frenzy and swishing their long ochre-stained hair is no less impressive for that.

Leaving South Horr you're thrown out onto a blistering plain of shimmering heat and chunks of black lava. Ahead, the dark outline of Mount Kulal offers the only relief from this desolate landscape. Camel trains carrying goods from the north and east may be spotted in the distance. The road seems to go on for ever until suddenly it swings left and dips, revealing the silver glimmer of Lake Turkana before you. Surrounded by total desolation it seems incredible that so much water can exist in so arid a place. In fact the lake is fed by only one river (which flows in from the northern end in Ethiopia). Once it stretched south to Lake Baringo but slowly it's shrinking. Depending on the light it can appear silver, pale blue, granite grey and occasionally the colour of jade, hence its name – the Jade Sea. A rough track bumps downhill before winding along the lake shore to Loyangalani.

515 km – Loyangalani (see **A-Z**). A mass of corrugated-iron shacks and dried-mud huts. There is an Italian mission close to the Oasis Lodge where you may be able to buy petrol (expensive). For those on the overland trucks or coming by car you'll stay in the Sunset Camp which is backed by palm trees, surrounded by a fence, and may have sodas for sale. Otherwise the only other accommodation is the pricey Oasis Lodge. Activities in Loyangalani are likely to include a visit to the el-Molo tribe just north of the town. The smallest tribe in Kenya, the el-Molo live off fishing the lake and charging tourists to see their village. Increasing intermarriage with the Turkana (see **Tribes**) means the pure bloodlines of this tiny tribe are close to extinction. Otherwise you are limited to swimming in the lake (watch out for crocodiles), buying fish for dinner or just simply absorbing the extraordinary landscape and atmosphere of the Jade Sea. You may be able to arrange a fishing trip through the lodge or by coming to an arrangement with one of the villagers. From Loyangalani backtrack to Maralal and Kisima and follow the road to the Samburu Game Reserve. From there continue south to Nanyuki and Nairobi.

Aberdares: Situated 155 km north of Nairobi, the Aberdares are a range of rolling highlands, dropping on the west into the Rift Valley (see **A-Z**) and on the east side facing towards Mount Kenya (see **A-Z**). Once known as the White Highlands and, since independence, the Aberdare Range, they rise to approximately 2800 m. These lush mountains and the areas around drew the early white settlers and became the farming heartland of the colony. In earlier times they formed part of the homelands of the Kikuyu (see **Tribes**) but today much of the Aberdares have been incorporated into the national park. See GAME PARKS-ABERDARE.

Accidents & Breakdowns: In the event of an accident in a hired car (see **Car Hire**) you should have paid the collision damage waiver to the rental firm which covers you for damage. Exchange names, addresses and insurance details with the other party. If anyone has been injured in the accident, call the police (see **A-Z**). If you break down most towns and garages will have a mechanics shop where all but the most terminal faults can be repaired. However, negotiate a price before the work is carried out. If you are a member of a motoring organization check with them about additional insurance and reciprocal arrangements with the Automobile Association of Kenya. See **Driving, Embassies & Consulates, Emergency Number**.

Accommodation: There is a wide choice of accommodation in Kenya, ranging from the luxurious and expensive to the basic and cheap, with everything else in between. The better hotels and lodges (see GAME PARKS) are classified with a star rating system running from the best at five star down to one star. In the high season (Dec.-Mar.,

July-Aug.) it is advisable to book the good hotels and lodges well in advance. Costs vary widely, but for a good medium-priced hotel you can expect to pay £20-30 per night. In the low season (April-May, Sep.-Nov.) many hotels offer discounts. Nairobi and Mombasa are full of booking agencies and tour operators (see **Guides**) who will arrange accommodation for you if you have not already booked. See **Camping**, **Youth Hostels**.

Adamson, George & Joy: The husband and wife team who devoted their lives to the big cats of Africa and were made famous by the book and film *Born Free*, which traced the life of Elsa the lioness (see NAIROBI-EXCURSION 3). Their work brought early interest and concern for Kenya's wildlife, and Samburu, Buffalo Springs and Shaba reserves (see GAME PARKS-SAMBURU) were all created as a result of their work. Although they separated, the couple continued to work with the big cats. Joy was murdered in 1980 in Shaba while George was killed in 1989 by bandits.

Airports: There are two international airports in Kenya. Jomo Kenyatta International Airport lies within a 30 min drive of Nairobi city centre. Airport facilities include a bank, car-hire offices (see **A-Z**), an information desk, a duty-free shop and restaurants. Buses (see **A-Z**) and taxis (see **A-Z**) run to and from the city centre. Moi International Airport on the coast serves Mombasa and has similar facilities. On departure from Kenya travellers should note that there is a departure tax of US$20 which must be paid in cash (traveller's cheques are not acceptable). This can be paid in other currencies, but not Kenya shillings (see **Currency**). All the major airline companies have offices in Nairobi and are represented at the airports. Both these airports also handle internal flights and Kenya Airways runs scheduled flights daily from Jomo Kenyatta Airport to Kisumu, Malindi and Mombasa.
A number of private companies run services to a wide range of destinations round the country from Wilson Airport, Nairobi. Air Kenya Aviation, tel: Nairobi 501421, operates perhaps the most extensive service. Both Air Kenya and private companies run equivalent services from Moi International Airport. Travel agents in Nairobi and Mombasa

will be able to advise you which companies fly where and when. See **Charter Aircraft**.

Amboseli: Overshadowed by Kilimanjaro (see **A-Z**), this park lies 190 km from Nairobi on Kenya's southern border with Tanzania. While not one of the largest national parks (see **A-Z**), Amboseli does offer a wide range of wildlife, much of which can be easily spotted due to the flat grassland terrain. In recent years increased tourism and off-track driving has caused considerable

damage to the park's delicate ecosystem. Amboseli is part of the Masai (see **Tribes**) heartland and the tribespeople can be seen herding their cattle around the park's perimeter and sometimes in the park itself. See GAME PARKS-AMBOSELI.

Arab Influence: From the 8thC, Arabs from the Gulf and Persia made the long journey across the Indian Ocean and traded with the inhabitants on the coast of East Africa. As a result of this trade and subsequent intermarriage, the Swahili culture was heavily influenced in language, literature and religion by the Arabs. Today the coastal population is predominantly Muslim and much of the architecture, particularly in Mombasa Old Town (see MOMBASA-WHAT TO SEE, **Mombasa**) and Lamu (see MOMBASA-EXCURSION 2, **A-Z**), is Islamic.

Baby-sitters: There are no baby-sitting facilities other than those which your hotel may be able to offer. See **Children**.

Banks: See **Currency**, **Money**, **Opening Times**.

Best Buys: Finding items to buy is the least of the traveller's problems in Kenya. Almost everywhere you go there will be stalls and craftsmen only too eager to sell you wood and soapstone carvings, bracelets, necklaces and baskets. A lot of the goods are mass-produced in cooperative workshops and the quality varies enormously. However, you can't go far wrong with the brightly coloured woven baskets. The cheapest are made of plastic so look carefully for those woven from sisal and wool. Wood and soapstone carved figurines can make attractive ornaments though it really comes down to personal taste. Beaten-metal bracelets and earrings are endemic throughout the country and can be excellent and inexpensive purchases. Another good buy are the brightly coloured kangas (wrapround sarong-like lengths of cotton) worn by women, while for men there are the more conservatively patterned kikois. Both are ideal for beach wear. In all cases always bargain hard for items. The initial figure quoted will almost invariably be at least double the going rate and often considerably more. See MOMBASA-SHOPPING, NAIROBI-SHOPPING, **Markets**, **Shopping**.

Bicycle & Motorcycle Hire: Neither bicycle nor motorcycle hire are common as yet in Kenya, primarily because neither form of vehicle is permitted in the game parks (see GAME PARKS). Some hotels on the coast hire out bicycles to guests.

Bird-watching: There are more than 1200 species of bird in Kenya and even a basic knowledge will greatly enhance your visit. John Williams' *Field Guide to the Birds of East and Central Africa* (HarperCollins) is the classic on the subject. For the enthusiast, British groups organize ornithological safaris to Kenya, while in Nairobi, the Museum Ornithology Society organizes bird-watching trips round the city environs for a small donation. Telephone the National Museum for more details. Birdlife can be found in almost every part of the country but certainly not to be missed are the lakes of Naivasha, Nakuru (see **NAIROBI-EXCURSION 3**), Bogoria (see **A-Z**) and Baringo (see **A-Z**).

Blixen, Karen (1885-1962): The Danish writer came to Kenya and lived on a farm outside Nairobi. The suburb which has been absorbed by the city today bears her name (see **Nairobi**). She became very much part of the colonial establishment but after her lover, Denis Finch-Hatton, died in a plane crash she left Kenya, never to return. Her book, *Out of Africa*, written under her pseudonym Isak Dinesen, captures much of the atmosphere of those colonial times and was subsequently made into an Oscar-winning film starring Meryl Streep and Robert Redford. The Karen Blixen Museum is situated, as you would expect, in the restored farmhouse in Karen.

A–Z

Budget: Basic commodities are relatively cheap in Kenya. However, once you start paying for safaris and the like, costs rise substantially. High rates of inflation are reflected by ever-increasing prices and costs given in this book may well be subject to upward revision.

Breakfast	Kshs 30
Lunch	Kshs 40
Dinner	Kshs 100
Beer	Kshs 30
Soft drinks	Kshs 8
Game parks	Ksh 220

Buses: These fall into two main categories: those that run between towns throughout the country and those that serve the cities of Nairobi and Mombasa. There are several major companies that run scheduled services between Nairobi and Mombasa, the best being Coast Bus and OTC. Alternatively, you can take the 'country buses' that travel between most towns. There are no timetables but most depart fairly regularly. It's simply a matter of asking around for when and where they go from. The locals will be only too happy to help. Kombi vans (covered vans with a raised sunroof) and *matatus* (see **A-Z**) undertake shorter journeys, are invariably packed, travel at heart-stopping speeds, and give a unique and fascinating travel experience. In and around both Nairobi and Mombasa there are local KBS buses and the ubiquitous *matatus*. As with the longer-distance buses, there are no set timetables – just ask around to find out which buses go where.

Cameras & Photography: Film is expensive in Kenya so it's advisable to bring all you'll need. Developing and printing is also expensive and it is best to wait until you get home. If you're planning to photograph wildlife you'll need a telephoto or 200 mm lens. Dust and heat are a problem so keep your equipment in bags when not in use, and

keep film out of direct sunlight and places where it's likely to overheat.
If taking photos of people, it is both polite and politic to ask permission
first. Tribespeople (see **Tribes**) who are wise to the tourists' ways are
likely to demand a small fee – around Kshs 20 is reasonable. Taking
photographs of police, soldiers, the President (see **Moi**) and the national flag is prohibited; equally airports, bridges, army barracks, etc. are
sensitive subjects and it is advisable not to photograph these.

Camping: Camping in Kenya is different and exciting, carrying with it
the romantic aura of Old Africa. There's a tremendous sense of wilderness and closeness to nature which just isn't captured by lodges and
hotels, however good. Finding sites is rarely a problem, especially on
safari (see **A-Z**), as all the game parks will have some form of public
camp site (see GAME PARKS), while many hotels will also have discreet
facilities if you ask. Camping in and around Mombasa and Nairobi or
on the coastal beaches is less advisable due to the threat of robbery
(see **Crime & Theft**). On the equipment front, either bring your own
(mosquito netting is a 'must'), or if you are renting a car (see **Car Hire**)
some car-hire firms do camping packages that provide equipment with
the vehicle. Camping in the bush is probably not for the complete
novice, but the basic requirements are a tent, a cooking grill, pots,
pans, plates, cutlery, water carriers and a cool box. Check where you
pitch your tent to ensure it's not on an animal trail or you are liable to
find a hippo or the like trundling over you in the night (see **Wildlife**). A
fire is essential to keep animals away but make sure it's safe with a surround of stones to ensure it doesn't run out of control. Finally, remember to pitch your camp early as darkness falls with alarming speed.

Car Hire: Having your own vehicle is perhaps the best way to get out
and see Kenya, though it is an expensive option. There's a daily mini-
mum rental charge of about Kshs 500, plus a collision damage waiver,
effectively your insurance, at around Kshs 200 per day. On top of that
there's an additional charge of about Kshs 5 per kilometre. If you don't
have a credit card you'll also have to leave a deposit of approximately
Kshs 15,000 with the hire company. If hiring for a lengthy period, special rates can usually be negotiated. All the major hire companies oper-

ate out of Nairobi and Mombasa, including Avis, Hertz and Budget. Car reservations can be made through these companies before you arrive. If hiring once you've reached Kenya one of the cheapest companies is Payless Car Hire on Koinange St, Nairobi, tel: 338400. If you want to camp both Hertz, tel: 331960 and Habibs Cars, tel: 20463, in Nairobi run packages hiring out equipment with their vehicles (see **Camping**). Drivers must be over 23 and under 70 years of age and while a home driving licence can be used for up to three months in Kenya it is advisable and less hassle to have an international driving licence. Types of cars range from Land Rovers and Land Cruisers to the more regular, and cheaper, Suzuki and Toyota saloons. Depending on your planned route and weather conditions you will have to decide whether two-wheel or four-wheel drive is your best option. In the mid-price range Suzuki jeeps provide light four-wheeled drive transport though for more than two people they can be rather cramped. When you pick up your hire car check that you have a good spare tyre and a full complement of tools. It is also worth glancing over the engine to make sure there are no glaring deficiencies. See **Driving**.

Charter Aircraft: For large groups, or the very wealthy, chartering your own aircraft can be a viable proposition. Check with Wilson Airport in Nairobi and Moi International in Mombasa. See **Airports**.

Chemists: There is no shortage of chemists shops in Kenya. On the main street of every town and many villages you will find one selling a range of toiletries and medicines although often not the brands that you are used to. They are usually open 0800-1700/1800 Mon.-Fri. with an hour break for lunch. See **Health**.

Children: Kenya can be an excellent place to bring children. Hotels and restaurants admit children at any time of day and most will have children's menus and other facilities available. However, ensure with your doctor that they are adequately protected against tropical diseases, particularly malaria. Also remember that Kenya spans the equator and that even when it doesn't feel hot the sun can burn vigorously, so bring the appropriate protective creams and clothing (see **Health**).

Climate: Situated on the equator, it is altitude rather than seasons that tends to effect temperatures and Kenya has a pleasant warm climate with two rainy seasons, one in April and May, the other in Oct. and Nov. The hottest months are Dec., Jan., Feb. and Mar., with temperatures on the coast averaging 28-32°C and 24-26°C in Nairobi. June, July and Aug. are the coolest months. Around Nairobi and up in the Aberdares (see **A-Z**) it can get surprisingly cold, particularly at night, while on the coast high humidity can make it stiflingly hot. Everywhere, regardless of the actual heat, the sun has the capacity to burn (see **Health**).

Coffee: Kenyan coffee is famous all over the world and it plays a vital part in the country's economy, amounting to around one-third of all exports. As such, changes in the world market price for coffee have a strong impact on the country as shown by the boom and then slump of the mid-late 1970s. Coffee demands very specific soil and climatic conditions and some parts of Kenya fulfill these demands perfectly, largely around Mount Kenya (see **A–Z**). There are still large coffee plantations but a significant proportion of the coffee crop now comes from small-holdings rather than large plantations. You can enjoy the coffee at its freshest in any one of the numerous cafés and coffee shops in Nairobi.

Complaints: In the better hotels, restaurants and lodges, you can expect to find complaints dealt with effectively. However, as the prices you pay drop so does the service you receive. Always weigh up the potential hassle against the problem you want rectified.

Conversion Chart:

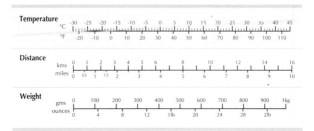

Credit Cards: See **Money**.

Crime & Theft: There are a lot of comparatively wealthy tourists in Kenya, and a lot of poor people, so it is not surprising that theft is fairly common – especially in the major cities and tourist destinations. It's not something to become paranoid about but you should certainly be aware of the risks. It is inadvisable to walk around Nairobi after dark,

though Mombasa is somewhat safer. If you are visiting poorer parts of the city, or busy markets (see **A-Z**), do not carry large sums of money; just take what you need and leave the rest in the hotel safe. Keep cameras in a bag unless using them and watch all your possessions all the time. Be aware of your surrounding circumstances, avoiding alleyways and the like where muggings could take place. If you do get mugged it's safest not to resist. Decide whether the amounts stolen make the hassle of going to the police worthwhile. It's not unknown for thieves to be shot by the police in the act of apprehension. If you need a police report for insurance purposes remember that politeness in the face of officialdom can go a long way. If a serious offence has taken place contact your embassy/consulate (see **A-Z**). See **Emergency Number**, **Insurance**, **Police**.

Currency: The Kenyan shilling (Kshs) is the national unit of currency. Each shilling breaks down into 100 cents. Banknotes are Kshs 10, 20, 50, 100 and 200. Coins are Kshs 1, 5 and 50c (silver), and 5 and 10c (copper). People often refer to shillings as 'bob'. See **Money**.

Customs: On the whole, Kenya and Kenyans are so laid-back as to be almost horizontal! However, there are a few points of etiquette to bear in mind. Kenya has a large Muslim community and if you are visiting mosques it is polite to ask the guardian if you can go inside. Remember to take your shoes off and make sure you are properly dressed. While people on the coast are particularly used to tourists, nude or topless sunbathing is not approved of. Tribespeople are often wary of having their photograph taken – it's polite to ask permission first – and you may have to pay for the privilege (see **Cameras & Photography**). With its colonial past and less than liberal government it's probably wise to keep conversations and comments away from domestic politics.

Customs Allowances:

Duty Free Into:	Cigarettes	*or*	Cigars	*or*	Tobacco	Spirits		Wine
KENYA	200		*or*		0.5lb	1 bottle	*or*	1 bottle
UK	200		50		250 g	1*l*		2*l*

Dentists: In emergencies there are dentists in both Nairobi and Mombasa but, if possible, you will be better off and safer if you can wait until you return home. Transmission of AIDS is a risk to keep in mind. If you are planning a long stay it is well worth a visit to your own dentist before you leave. See **Health**.

Diani: See MOMBASA-EXCURSION 3.

Disabled People: Kenya has little in the way of facilities for disabled people. That said, most game lodges are built at ground level and so are accessible, and you can be sure that there will always be plenty of people around to lend a hand. However, it would be wise to advise your tour company/hotel of any special requirements beforehand. It's safer to take an adequate supply of medicines with you rather than to rely on their local availability. See **Health**.

Drinks: Lager-type beers are the most common and popular of Kenyan alcoholic beverages. White Cap, Tusker and Pilsner are the predominant brands and are all pretty similar. You can also get Guinness. On the spirits front both gin and vodka are produced locally, though for the rest you'll have to rely on more expensive imports. Wine is also mostly imported and expensive, although a rather unusual papaya wine is worth a try. Soft drinks are widely available and cheap. Tap water in the main towns is drinkable, elsewhere rely on bottled or boiled water. As you would expect in Kenya, tea and coffee are available everywhere and delicious since both are home-grown (see **Coffee**, **Tea**).

Driving: Driving is on the left, although the majority of the country's roads are untarred so you will find yourself and other vehicles following the smoothest route. The speed limit is 100 kph. Don't assume anything about other traffic and be particularly wary of *matatus* (see **A-Z**) which travel at alarming speeds and have an unnerving tendency to pull out and stop unexpectedly. Always make sure you have a spare tyre as punctures are regular occurences. If travelling in game parks (see GAME PARKS, **National Parks & Reserves**) or less inhabited areas it's worth carrying a jerry can of fuel, and if you do have a puncture or breakdown keep an eye open for wild animals. Other vehicles will usually stop to assist if you are in trouble. Before setting off on a journey, especially in the rainy season, it's advisable to check whether your intended route is passable. Night driving cannot be recommended. If travelling independently make sure you have a good road map, though on the whole the roads are well signposted throughout the country. Many of Kenya's roads are extremely rough so drive carefully to avoid damage to both yourself and your vehicle. It's worth checking over your car before each day's drive to ensure there are no obvious problems. Breakdowns are no fun at the best of times and one out in the bush could leave you stranded for some considerable time. See **Accidents & Breakdowns**, **Car Hire**, **Insurance**, **Petrol**.

Drugs: The use or possession of drugs is illegal and you're unlikely to receive sympathetic treatment if you are caught. Marijuana is fairly widely available, especially down at the coast, though police are making efforts to clamp down. *Miraa*, which looks like green twigs, is a legal stimulant most commonly chewed by truck and bus drivers with either coke or bubble gum to keep them awake.

Eating Out: Eating out in Kenya can be anything you want it to be from excellent and expensive (by local standards) to cheap and cheerful. In Nairobi, particularly, you can find most types of cuisine from African and Asian to Greek, French and Italian. At the bottom end of the market in the smaller cafés the choice will tend to be limited to Asian (curries, samosa, etc., some of it excellent) and African (meat or vegetables with ugali, a maize porridge). Breakfasts are usually standard English cooked or cereal, fruit and toast. Only on the coast are you likely to find authentic Kenyan food, which tends to be fish and vegetable dishes cooked in coconut milk. In general, there are no set opening times for the majority of restaurants (which will be open for lunch, evening meal, etc.), unless they are in hotels which may have more regular opening hours. As a rough guide to the costs of meals, you can expect to pay Kshs 200 plus (expensive), Kshs 80-100 (moderate) and Kshs 30-40 (inexpensive). See **MOMBASA-RESTAURANTS**, **NAIROBI-RESTAURANTS**, **Food**, **Tipping**.

Eldoret: 311 km northwest of Nairobi, and situated on the A 104 road through western Kenya to Uganda, Eldoret is a somewhat sleepy but friendly town on the fertile Uasin Gishu plateau. Originally named Eldare, meaning 'river', a misspelling in the *Official Gazette of Kenya* left the town with its current name. Facilities in the town include accommodation, banks, car hire and a post office. Trains running from Nairobi to Uganda also stop at Eldoret. See **NAIROBI-EXCURSION 4**.

Electricity: 240 volts. Three-pin 13 amp plugs are used. Lodges with their own generators may have different voltages though they will usually have adapters if asked.

Eliye Springs: Situated on the western shore of Lake Turkana (see **NAIROBI-EXCURSION 5**, **A-Z**) and reached by following the A 1 north from Kitale (see **A-Z**) to Lodwar and then following the B 4 to the lakeside. Eliye Springs was once a lodge but today is just a camp site. A little further north on the same road is Ferguson's Gulf, where you will find the Lake Turkana Angling Lodge. Fishing trips, not surprisingly, can be arranged. Game fishing (see **Fishing**) on Lake Turkana is reputed to be some of the best in the world, though beware of the crocodiles and hippos if you fancy a dip.

Embassies & Consulates:

UK – Bruce House, Standard St, PO Box 30465, Nairobi, tel: 335944.
Rep. of Ireland – Monrovia St, PO Box 30659, Nairobi, tel: 26771.
USA – Moi Ave, PO Box 30137, Nairobi, tel: 334141.
Australia – Development House, Moi Ave, PO Box 30360, Nairobi,
tel: 334666.
Canada – Comcraft House, Haile Selassie Ave, PO Box 30481, Nairobi,
tel: 334033.

Emergency Number:

Police, fire, ambulance   999

Events: There are few national events in Kenya's annual calendar. Top
of the bill is undoubtedly the Safari Rally (see **Sports**) which takes place
over Easter from Good Fri. through to Easter Mon. The cars make a
grand tour of Kenya's roughest roads at horrifying speeds. Further
details can be obtained from the AA in Nairobi. In the spring, Ramadan
may have some effect on your travels, especially on the coast when
many businesses are closed during the day. See **Public Holidays**.

Exploration: Inland Kenya avoided the attentions of the colonial powers until the mid-19thC as the slavers, traders and missionaries initially concentrated on the coastal strip. As well as disease and unknown territory for those that dared venture inland, there was the additional deterrent of the Masai (see **Tribes**). Yet with much of Africa rife with European explorers, Kenya's turn was quick to come. It was not until the Masai were weakened by internal struggles in the latter part of the century that the British were able to construct their Mombasa to Uganda railway and open the region to full colonization. Despite the rigours of exploration a number of European missionaries and adventurers did launch expeditions inland. Among them were Dr Ludwig Krapf, a German missionary who first founded missions on the coast and then pushed further inland. His reports of finding a snow-capped mountain on the equator were dismissed as fanciful in Europe. Those early detractors are long gone but Mt Kenya (see **A-Z**) remains. Johannes Rebmann was another German missionary who worked with Krapf. He noted, and feared, the wildlife in the interior, particularly in the area that is today Tsavo National Park (see **GAME PARKS-TSAVO**). In

1848 he became the first European to reach Kilimanjaro (see **A-Z**). Joseph Thomson was a Scot who traversed Kenya via the Aberdares (see **GAME PARKS-ABERDARE**, **A-Z**), which he named after the President of the Royal Geographical Society, and the Rift Vallley (see **A-Z**) to reach Lake Victoria (see **A-Z**) in 1883 at the tender age of 24. He gave his name to the Thomson's gazelle (see **Wildlife**) and to Thomson's Falls. He survived countless encounters with the Masai and in one renowned instance diffused a threatening situation by removing his false teeth! Count Teleki was an Austrian explorer who, in 1888, was the first European to reach Lake Turkana (see **A-Z**). He named it Lake Rudolf, the name being changed after independence in 1963.

Fishing: The Kenyan coast has some of the world's best big game fishing. The main areas north of Mombasa are at Malindi (see **A-Z**), Lamu (see **A-Z**) and Kilifi and to the south at Shimoni and from the Diani Beach hotels (see **MOMBASA-EXCURSION 3**). Fishing occurs throughout the year though it is best from Sep.-Mar. Inland, rivers are predominantly fished for trout, especially in the Aberdares (see **A-Z**) and around Mount Kenya (see **A-Z**). See **Eliye Springs**.

Food: Most types of food are available in Kenya, given the country's multiracial mix. The Western palate is amply provided for, particularly in the tourist resorts. However, as soon as you leave those enclaves African and Asian food predominates. The following are typical: ugali – a thick white porridge made from maize, which is usually eaten as an accompaniment to meat stews or vegetables; *irio* – chickpeas, maize and potatoes mashed together and again eaten as an accompaniment; *sukuma wiki* – a spinach-like vegetable mixed with meat; samosa – a meat-filled pastry, often spicy, that has been deep-fried; *maharagway* – beans cooked in coconut milk; matoke – plantains (similar to bananas) steamed and served in coconut milk; *maandazi* – very similar to a doughnut but without the sugar coating, eaten with tea or coffee, often for breakfast; *chai* – tea made by boiling water, milk, sugar and tea together at the same time. An abundance of fruits is to be found in Kenya, ranging from familiar bananas, avocados, tangerines and pineapples to the more distinctly tropical mangoes, papaya, custard apples, guavas and passion fruit. Overindulgence or eating fruit you haven't peeled yourself can have unpleasant side effects (see **Health**). See MOMBASA-RESTAURANTS, NAIROBI-RESTAURANTS, **Eating Out**.

Fort Jesus: The fort is situated in the eastern part of Mombasa, close to the Old Town. The Portuguese, who had made a number of prior sorties to Mombasa and other settlements along the East African coast, started the building of Fort Jesus in 1593. It soon became the focal point for control of the region. As the Omani Empire grew more powerful and established trading links and control of the coastal strip, so the influence of the Portuguese waned until in 1698, after over a year's siege, the fort fell to the Arabs. Thirty years later the African population revolted, allowing the Portuguese to retake the fort – only to be forced out again by the Arabs, this time for good. The new Omani rulers, the Mazni family, soon declared their own independence from Oman and governed coastal Kenya for the next hundred years. However, in the 1820s the Omani Arabs, with British backing, regained control of the coast and the fort. With the coming of the British colo-

nization of Kenya in the late 19thC the fort fell under British control and became the town prison, which it remained until 1958. The fort today contains a museum which recounts the history and culture of coastal Kenya, together with an Omani house which has been restored. The fort was effectively a town and you can see it's ruined church, streets, toilets and great halls. See **MOMBASA-WHAT TO SEE**, **Mombasa**.

Game Parks: See **GAME PARKS**, **National Parks & Reserves**.

Gedi: Gedi is an excellently-preserved example of a 15thC Swahili town whose architecture displays the inevitable Arab influence (see **A-Z**). It seems that Gedi was never discovered by the Portuguese who inhabited the nearby port of Malindi (see **A-Z**), just to the south of Gedi, during the same period. It was not until the 17thC that the town was abandoned. In its heyday Gedi would have been a walled-in town housing a population of over 2000 in primarily mud and thatch huts. Today the central attractions of the ruins are the palace and the mosque, and these and the other remains give an idea of what life must have been like in a medieval Swahili town. See **MOMBASA-EXCURSION 1**.

Guides: For most visitors to Kenya the only real need they have for a guide is when they go on safari (see **A-Z**). Unless you are hiring a vehicle and driving yourself, when you can usually pick up a game-park guide at the lodges and in and around the parks (see **GAME PARKS**), your guide is more likely to come in the form of a safari tour operator. Both Nairobi and Mombasa are packed with tour operators only too eager to arrange your game-park safari. This will usually include transport there and back, accommodation and game drives round the park. Prices vary hugely depending on how you travel, where you stay and for how long. The following is a selection of tour operators: UTC, corner of Muindi Mbingu St and Kaunda St, Nairobi, tel: 331960 and Moi Ave, Mombasa, tel: 316333/4; Safaricentre, Nairobi Hilton, Nairobi, tel: 24885 and Kenyatta Ave (near 680 Hotel), Mombasa, tel: 315285; Safari Camp Services, Koinange St, Nairobi, tel: 330130/28936.

Health: There is both public and private medical care available in Kenya. However, it is advisable, if at all possible, to try and wait until you get home for treatment, other than in an emergency. You will have to pay for any treatment on the spot and claim it back on your insur-

ance later. It is also advisable to have injections for cholera, typhoid, tetanus and polio before entering Kenya and, unless coming from an infected area, inoculation against yellow fever is still to be recommended. It is also probably wise to have an injection of gamma globulin against hepatitis before departure. Malaria is probably the greatest health risk in Kenya, especially on the coast, so ensure you have a full supply of malaria tablets to cover both your trip and a six-week period after you return home. Your doctor will advise you as to the current anti-resistant varieties. The tablets aside, protect yourself against being bitten by the disease-carrying mosquitoes by sleeping under a mosquito net, burning mosquito coils and applying insect repellent, particularly at dusk and after nightfall. If you find yourself feeling feverous, with headaches and flu-like symptoms, consult a doctor immediately. If untreated malaria can kill. Avoid swimming in lakes and rivers as most are contaminated with bilharzia, a parasitic fluke that lives in freshwater snails. Leaving the snail the flukes burrow into humans and animals to reproduce in the bloodstream. The disease is curable but rather unpleasant. Diarrhoea and dysentery are commonly caused by drinking impure water (tap water is generally safe), or from salads or pre-peeled fruit. Going without food for a day and drinking plenty of safe fluids will normally see it off. If the symptoms persist consult a doctor. The sun causes a surprising number of problems from sunburn to heat rashes and sunstroke, so be conscious of its effects and protect yourself with creams, hats, etc. Sexually-transmitted diseases are widespread and notably AIDS has a very high incidence in East Africa. It is not predominantly confined to the drug-using and homosexual communities; around 80% of prostitutes are believed to be infected and Kenya has large numbers of both male and female prostitutes. Casual sex is a highly dangerous diversion in this part of the world. The main hospitals are: Nairobi – The Kenyatta National Hospital, tel: 334800; Nairobi Hospital (private), tel: 722160. Mombasa – The Coast General Hospital, tel: 314201; The Katherine Bibby Hospital, tel: 312191. See **Chemists**, **Emergency Number**, **Insurance**.

Hell's Gate: Close to Lake Naivasha (see **A-Z**), Hell's Gate is a dramatic narrow gorge (can be traversed on foot), volcanic in origin, that

cuts west from Naivasha and stretches out to the north of the road to Narok. The area is a breeding ground for vultures, eagles and buzzards. In 1882 the German explorer Gustav Fischer's expedition was ambushed by Masai (see **Tribes**) here; few of the party survived. See **NAIROBI-EXCURSION 3**.

Hitchhiking: Hitching is certainly feasible in Kenya though with frequent cheap buses (see **A-Z**) available it is hardly essential. Additionally, on the majority of roads there is not exactly a surfeit of traffic. However, people are often willing to stop. It's good practice to offer the driver a little money. Note: it might be unwise to hitch on your own. Standing at the roadside for lengthy periods in certain areas may be asking for trouble.

Insurance: You should take out travel insurance covering you against theft, loss of property and medical expenses (including repatriation) for the duration of your trip. Your insurance company or travel agent will be able to advise you on the most suitable policy. See **Car Hire**, **Crime & Theft**, **Health**.

Jumba la Mtwana: Just north of Mombasa (see **A-Z**), Jumba la Mtwana is the site of another 15thC village. It is smaller than Gedi (see **A-Z**) but there are two ruined mosques in the settlement, one situated by the sea. From the village it's an easy walk onto Jumba beach where you can sunbathe and swim. See **MOMBASA-EXCURSION 1**.

Kakamega Forest: The only rainforest in Kenya is situated on the road between Kitale (see **A-Z**) and Kisumu (see **A-Z**) forest. A tangle of immense trees, vines and undergrowth inhabited by a wide and exotic range of birdlife make Kakamega a real jungle and a delight for ornithologists (see **Bird-watching**). See **NAIROBI-EXCURSION 4**.

Karen: See **NAIROBI-EXCURSION 2**, **Blixen**, **Nairobi**.

Kenyatta, Jomo (1892-1978): As the first President of independent Kenya, Jomo Kenyatta holds a special place in the affections of most Kenyans. He was born in the Kikuyu homelands (see **Tribes**), the son of a poor farmer, and worked his way up from his humble roots, starting with an education at a Church of Scotland Mission School. He later moved to Nairobi and became involved with nationalist politics, changing his name from Johnstone Kamau to Jomo Kenyatta. He continued to study, in London and Moscow, and on his return to Kenya after World War II, became leader of the Kenyan African Union (KAU) and the recognized head of the Kenyan independence movement. In 1952, during the Mau Mau (see **A-Z**) rebellion, Kenyatta was arrested, tried and convicted on the somewhat tenuous evidence that he was one of the Mau Mau's leaders. On his release seven years later he returned to politics to lead the Kenyan African National Union (KANU) and became Kenya's first post-independence President in December 1963. Under Kenyatta's leadership Kenya became one of Africa's most stable and successful countries. Kenyatta had espoused the notion of harambee (pulling together) against the evils of tribalism and succeeded in changing his nation from a colony to an independent republic with few of the teething problems found elsewhere on the continent. He died in 1978 amid complaints of corruption and political abuse which quickly turned to an outpouring of national grief and nostalgia for the man who had figured so prominently in Kenya's independence struggle. He was succeeded by Daniel arap Moi (see **A-Z**).

Kericho: 265 km northwest of Nairobi. Kericho lies at the centre of Kenya's profitable and extensive tea-growing area (see **Tea**). The combination of warm days and wet afternoons, as well as a suitable altitude for growing tea, make this ideal plantation territory. Once dominated totally by European settlers, some of the lands have been distributed to smaller local farmers, although it is now the large international conglomerates that own the huge plantations which remain. The town itself is attractive enough, with most of the activity taking place round the central square, although there is less of the bustle found elsewhere in Kenya as much of the local population lives out on the estates. See **NAIROBI-EXCURSION 4**.

Kikuyu: See **Tribes**

Kilimanjaro: Kilimanjaro is the highest mountain in Africa (5895 m) and although you can get spectacular views from Kenya, it actually lies in Tanzania. Volcanically formed, it has three peaks of which Uhuru (formally known as Kibo) is the highest. It is permanently capped with snow and even today it's not difficult to see why Johannes Rebmann (see **Exploration**), the first white man to discover the mountain, in 1848, was disbelieved when he reported its presence just south of the equator. Kilimanjaro's first European conqueror was Hans Mayer who reached the summit in 1892, although it is said that King Solomon's son, Menelik, went to die there. Today, ascents of Kilimanjaro can be made from Tanzania and for the Kenya tourist the mountain makes a spectacular backdrop to Amboseli National Park (see **GAME PARKS-AMBOSELI**).

Kisumu: 250 km northwest of Nairobi. The main attraction of Kisumu has to be Lake Victoria (see **A-Z**), on whose shores the town stands. The town is Kenya's third largest although recent years have seen something of a commercial slump. It's a pleasant laid-back place, retaining an aura of times past, and makes an excellent base from which to explore western Kenya. In colonial times it was at the hub of all transport routes through East Africa, with attendant administration and military installations, and accordingly had a large European community. Kisumu houses what is probably Kenya's best museum with good displays examining the wildlife and peoples of the region. There is an excellent market by the bus station. See **NAIROBI-EXCURSION 4**.

Kitale: 380 km northwest of Nairobi, Kitale stands at the foot of Mount Elgon (see **A-Z**) amid lush grassland. It's an attractive town with reasonable accommodation. It was once a slaving base on the way to the coast but really came into its own with the arrival of the railway and settlers in 1925. Thereafter it developed into a prime agricultural region. Kitale has a fine museum, something of a feature in the towns of western Kenya. See **NAIROBI-EXCURSION 4**.

Lake Baringo: A 2 hr drive north of Lake Nakuru (see **A-Z**) on the B 4, Lake Baringo is renowned for its fabulous birdlife. Some 450 species of birds have been identified round the lake (see **Bird-watching**). Crocodile and hippo can also be seen in its waters. There is lodge accommodation both on the lakeshore and out on Island Camp in the lake's centre.

Lake Bogoria: Follow the B 4 as if travelling to Lake Baringo (see **A-Z**) but turn off at Mogotio. The rough road drops down to the lakeshore through dry sisal estates. The lake stands at just 963 m above sea level and accordingly it gets extremely hot during the day. The lake itself has a green tinge from the algae in its waters which attract huge numbers of flamingos to feed round its shores. To the west of the lake are hot springs.

Lake Naivasha: North of Nairobi off the A 104. Another idyll for birdlife (see **Bird-watching**), the lake and surrounding lands are very beautiful and have long been a favoured retreat for Kenyans. Crescent Island out on the lake is a bird and wildlife sanctuary, its gazelles, monkeys and birds making it a delightful spot to wander around. In recent years the water level of the lake has dropped, connecting the island to the shore. See **NAIROBI-EXCURSION 3**.

Lake Nakuru: Famous for the vast numbers of pink flamingos which settle on the lakeshore, Nakuru, in fact, provides a habitat for a wide array of birds while the national park on its shores is an excellent place to spot antelope, baboons and monkeys. A reduction in the concentration of algae in the lake has meant that in the last decade more and more of the flamingos have gone north to Lake Bogoria (see **A-Z**). See **NAIROBI-EXCURSION 3**.

Lake Turkana: Formerly known as Lake Rudolf (see **Exploration**) and sometimes called the Jade Sea because of the green tinge caused by algae, Turkana lies surrounded by blazing volcanic desert. The heat is so intense that over 3 m of water evaporates from the lake's surface each year. It stretches for more than 250 km north to the Ethiopian border. In its alkaline waters Nile perch grow to huge sizes and crocodiles bask. The colour of the lake seems to change constantly, ranging from moody grey through blues and greens. The fishing is excellent but beware the storms that can blow up with alarming speed. See **NAIROBI-EXCURSION 5**.

Lake Victoria: The size of Ireland and the biggest freshwater lake in the world, Lake Victoria dominates Kenya's western border, although the largest part of it actually lies across in Tanzania and Uganda. It's waters provide food and until the disintegration of Uganda under Idi Amin it also provided a major transport route. Boat trips to and from Kenyan towns on its shores can be arranged and watching the sunsets over the lake is a 'must'. It is one of the sources of the Nile and was the heart of the obsession which gripped so many 18thC European explorers (see **Exploration**). See **NAIROBI-EXCURSION 4**.

Lamu: 225 km north of Malindi (see **A-Z**). Lying just off the coast, Lamu is both an island and the name of the main town. Perhaps more than anywhere else, Lamu reflects coastal Kenya's strong Islamic heritage with its mosques, whitewashed buildings, narrow streets, women covered and veiled by their buibui's and men in white muslin robes. Historically, Lamu's economy was based on slaving, right up to the end of the 19thC. However, when the British ended the trade the island's economy slumped and was only revived in the 1960s with the arrival of the first Western tourists. In the subsequent period Lamu became one of the great destinations among travellers. It's isolation from the rest of Kenya has preserved the laid-back atmosphere and fabulous architecture that make Lamu such a delight to visit. As if that wasn't enough of a draw Lamu also has some of the best and most undisturbed beaches in Kenya, though their discovery, in recent times, by tour operators make it a place to visit sooner rather than later. See **MOMBASA-EXCURSION 2**.

Language: Kenya has two official languages, English and Swahili, and you'll find that the majority of people speak at least some English.

In the major cities its usage predominates, though in more remote areas tribal dialects take over. The Swahili language is of coastal origin and is used as a lingua franca, enabling the various tribes to communicate outside their own dialects. It's not difficult to learn at least a few words and phrases (Swahili phrasebooks are widely available) and these will prove invaluable when away from the main centres. Generally, the words are pronounced as they read. Your efforts, however limited, will be well received by the locals.

Laundries: Kenya has no Launderettes as such, though the bigger towns are likely to have dry-cleaning shops. For everyday washing you'll find that most hotels, even the cheapest, will have some laundry service. However, the combination of enthusiastic scrubbing and paint-stripping washing powders can dramatically reduce the life of even the hardiest clothes. For delicate items handwashing them yourself is recommended.

Leakey, Louis (1903-72): The late Dr Leakey, the palaeontologist, his wife Mary and their son Richard, are well-known for their research into the origins and development of mankind and in particular for the discovery in Sibiloi National Park of the remains of a skull some 2.8 million years old which is thought to have belonged to modern man's earliest ancestors. The area has been called 'the cradle of mankind'. Richard Leakey is currently director of Kenya's National Museum (see **NAIROBI-WHAT TO SEE**) and at the forefront of Kenya's endeavours to curtail the activities of rhino and elephant poachers.

Lost Property: Being realistic, if you lose anything, unless it is in a lodge or up-market hotel, you're unlikely to recover it. Contacting the local police (see **A-Z**) may be necessary for the sake of insurance claims but weigh up the value of the mislaid item with the likely hassle. See **Insurance**.

Loyangalani: A small, dusty, fly-blown village on the eastern shores of Lake Turkana (see **A-Z**) inhabited by Turkana and Samburu tribespeople (see **Tribes**). It's the final stop for most visitors to the lake. There is a lodge on the outskirts of the village, a camp site and a mission station where it is possible to buy petrol (see **A-Z**). See NAIROBI-EXCURSION 5.

Malindi: 119 km north of Mombasa. This is one of Kenya's best-known beach resorts. Unlike the resorts to the south of Mombasa, it centres round a thriving town with a life of its own. Once a quiet, lazy place, it has today taken on a considerably more frenetic life style, though out of season it can still be extremely peaceful. There is plenty of accommodation in the town and this makes an excellent base from which to explore Watamu Marine National Park and the Gedi ruins (see **Gedi**), as well as a good stopover for those travelling overland to Lamu (see **A-Z**). See MOMBASA-EXCURSION 1.

Markets: Markets throughout Kenya are always worth a visit for their colour and atmosphere alone. Of course there are specific tourist markets, like the City Market in Nairobi, but the local produce markets are where you'll see the real Kenya at work. Remember to bargain for everything and don't be afraid to say no, but enjoy the sales patter and join in. If you are taking a camera be discreet and don't carry any more money than you'll need (see **Crime & Theft**). See MOMBASA-SHOPPING, NAIROBI-SHOPPING.

Matatus: These are privately operated vehicles, usually Kombi vans, which, like the buses, work both in and around towns and between towns. They are invariably packed to the gunwales so it's best if you can get in beside the driver. They are often the most effective or only transport around and they can be a fun experience, although they do travel at amazing speeds. Ask around for the part of town the *matatus* leave from (it's normally near the bus station) and then again for one going to your destination. They don't have regular departure times and only leave when they have a full complement of passengers, so if you don't want to wait around try to find one that's nearly full. See **Buses**.

Mau Mau (1952-56): The end of World War II found Kenyans pressing for land reform and increasingly the emergence of Kenyan nationalism (see **Kenyatta**). More radical elements, primarily from the Kikuyu tribe (see **Tribes**), formed an underground movement in the highlands north of Nairobi where members took oaths of allegiance against the British. In 1952 the government declared a state of emergency and banned all nationalist organizations. As British troops were sent out to the colony to deal with the revolt so the Mau Mau guerillas took to the forests, from where they launched attacks on both the British and those they deemed collaborators. Thousands of Kikuyu were detained in prison camps. By the end of the revolt in 1956 more than 13,000 Africans had died. It was the bloodiest period in Kenya's history and the vast majority of the population were caught between the two sides. Even today it remains a sensitive topic with Europeans and Africans alike.

Moi, Daniel arap: President of Kenya. President Moi succeeded Kenyatta (see **A-Z**) in 1978 and his slogan has been 'peace, love and unity'. He has argued consistently against the effects of tribalism. Moi comes from a small tribe, the Kalenjin, which to some extent has saved him from being labelled as partisan by the country's two largest tribes, the Luo and the Kikuyu (see **Tribes**). He survived a coup attempt by members of the air force in 1982 and again survived rioting and unrest in 1990. Calls for multi-party democracy have challenged his position once more and increasingly Kenya has found itself accused of human rights abuses.

Mombasa: 485 km southeast of Nairobi. As Kenya's second-largest city and major seaport Mombasa is not just, or even mainly, a tourist town, but rather a thriving trading centre with very much a life of its own. Set on an island surrounded by a natural harbour, it has inevitably had a central role in Kenya's coastal development. Arabs from Oman traded along the coast and established a base at Mombasa, where there is believed to have been some kind of settlement for around 2000 years. The Portuguese explorer Vasco da Gama landed here in 1498, and was followed by more Portuguese who ended up controlling the city and building Fort Jesus (see **A-Z**) in the process. Despite this European presence, until the late 17thC it was the Omani Arabs who really left their mark (see **Arab Influence**). Mombasa was the central trading post of their empire until 1832 when the Sultan of Muscat moved his court down the coast to Zanzibar. Thereafter the town

became something of a backwater until the British built the Uganda to Mombasa railway, making the town once more the hub of East Africa's trade. However, today it is the Arab influence that most noticeably remains, especially in the Old Town, with its narrow alleyways, ornate balconies, veiled women and kasbah atmosphere. The rest of the town is more familiar, with it's street markets, shops and restaurants. With a constant influx of both sailors and tourists it's hardly surprising that prostitution is rife – males will almost certainly be propositioned (see **Health**). For most people, any visit to the coast, whether arriving by plane, train or bus, usually starts in Mombasa, and while the town has the necessary facilities, it's rather chaotic, unruly atmosphere initially puts many off. However, for those that persevere the town has much to offer, presenting an Africa that many Westerners are unaware of. See **MOMBASA**.

Money: There is no restriction on the amount of money that can be brought into Kenya. However, on arrival you must fill out a currency declaration form on which you state how much money you are bringing. Each time you change money within the country this form must be stamped and you will receive a receipt which you should keep. On leaving Kenya this form will be inspected. You will be allowed to change money back as long as the form and receipts tally with your remaining cash. Although you will almost certainly be approached by black-market moneychangers it's not advisable to use them as, firstly, it is an offence for which you can be tried and deported and secondly, because you're more than likely to be swindled. Traveller's cheques are the best and safest method of carrying money. They can be exchanged at banks (0900-1400 Mon.-Fri., 0900-1100 Sat.) and at the main hotels and travel agents, although at a slightly lower rate. There are also bureaux de change in Nairobi and Mombasa. Changing money in banks can be a rather prolonged operation. The main banks are Standard Bank Ltd, Barclays Bank International and Kenya Commercial Bank, though there are many others. A branch of one of them can be found in most towns. In some Nairobi banks the foreign exchange counter stays open till 1630 and the bank at Jomo Kenyatta Airport (see **Airports**) is open 24 hr. Credit cards can be useful (particularly for flights and car hire – see **A-Z**). The ones most likely to be accepted are American Express, Visa and Access/Mastercard, in that order. Finally, when travelling out of the cities it's helpful to carry cash in small denominations as out in the bush getting change for large notes can be a problem. See **Crime & Theft**, **Currency**.

Mount Elgon: This mountain stands on the Kenya-Uganda border northwest of Nairobi and is 4321 m high with the highest point actually lying in Uganda. The Kenyan part of the mountain is designated a national park (see **A-Z**) and has a wide range of plant and animal life. See **NAIROBI-EXCURSION 4**.

Mount Kenya: Situated just north of the equator this is Kenya's highest mountain (5200 m) and the second highest in Africa (see **Kilimanjaro**). Ludwig Krapf (see **Exploration**) 'discovered' the mountain in 1849 and as with Rebmann's experience of Kilimanjaro the year before, found his reports of a snow-capped peak on the equator ridiculed in Europe. In fact the Kikuyu (see **Tribes**) had long known of its existence and believed that one of their gods, Ngai, lived on the summit. Situated about a 4 hr drive north of Nairobi, the mountain provides both excellent walking and serious climbing depending on which of its three peaks you aim at. It's surrounding slopes provide a home to a wide range of wildlife (see **A-Z**) and unusual vegetation. The mountain is frequently enveloped in cloud and your best chance of catching a glimpse of its striking summit is in the early hours of the morning. See **GAME PARKS-MT KENYA**.

Mount Kenya

Music: You'll hear a wide range of music in Kenya ranging from Swahili guitar music to more regular Western pop, from tribal drums to classical orchestrations. There isn't a great deal of public performance though you'll come across a little in Nairobi (see **NAIROBI-NIGHTLIFE**) and Mombasa or at tribal dance displays (see **NAIROBI-WHAT TO SEE**). Currently the most likely African music you'll hear in Kenya will have been inspired by bands from Zambia and Zaïre; occasionally bands from those countries will play certain venues in the main cities. If you want to buy albums the area around River Rd in Nairobi, where there are a number of small record shops, is probably your best bet. See **Nightlife**, **What's On**.

Mzima Springs: The springs (located in Tsavo National Park) consist of a number of pools fed with clear water from underground sources, and from here water is piped down to Mombasa. The springs draw large numbers of game to their waters and provide an excellent viewing point. See **GAME PARKS-TSAVO**.

Nairobi: 485 km northwest of Mombasa. Kenya's capital stands at an altitude of 1700 m so, despite lying just 140 km from the equator, it has a pleasant temperate climate throughout the year. It's current population is already over one million and rising fast. Most live in the suburbs

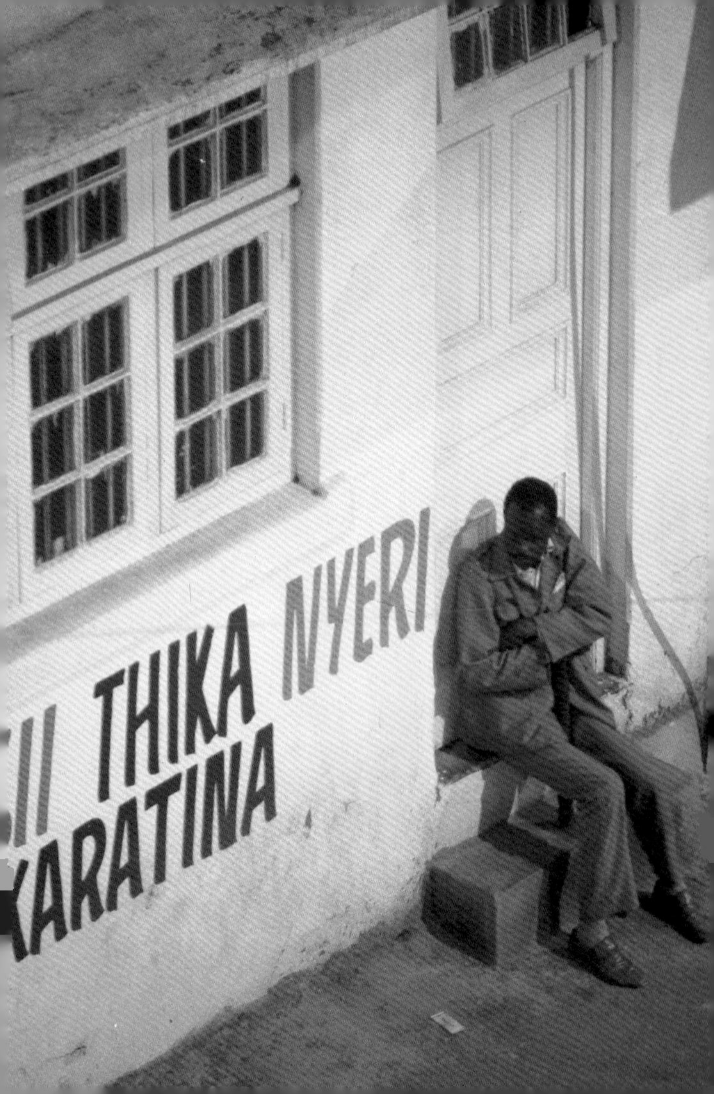
THIKA NYERI
KARATINA

and shanty towns that surround the city rather than in the centre itself,
which is a compact area largely made up of shops, offices, markets,
restaurants and hotels. Nairobi's roots lie in the building of the Uganda-
Mombasa railway, when it started life first as a construction camp and
then as a supply depot. Overcoming minor hiccups such as being burnt
down in 1902 to rid the settlement of a plague epidemic, it became the
capital of British East Africa in 1907. For many years it remained a
rather muddy colonial outpost, acting as a bureaucratic centre and supply town to the upcountry settlers. However, by the late 1920s the city
had begun to take shape and from there steadily built and developed to
its present position as East Africa's commercial capital. Today high-rise
blocks tower over the colonial remnants and the streets fairly bustle
with activity, yet much of the old atmosphere remains, as if you had
stepped back 20 years. The city is a cultural and ethnic hotchpotch
with representatives of all Kenya's tribes (see **A-Z**), plus a noticeable

foreign population derived from old colonial families, international businessmen and organizations, like the United Nations Development Programme, which are based in Nairobi. If the city centre becomes rather overpowering with its traffic and smog, a visit to the wealthier suburbs like Karen (see **Blixen**), Langata and Mutheiga (where the diplomatic community is largely based), can be a fascinating relief. There, amid the gorgeous tropical blooms that have given rise to one of Nairobi's nicknames, 'the city of flowers', are replicas of English country gardens. It's not hard to see why these suburbs have been described as a sort of 'tropical land', and if you were expecting the city to be very *Out of Africa* this is about as close as it gets. Finally, note that Nairobi has an unenviable reputation for street crime, much of it well-deserved, and walking around the town at night is not recommended (see **Crime & Theft**). See NAIROBI.

Nakuru: 156 km northwest of Nairobi. Nakuru is the fourth-largest town in Kenya and is a major supply post for the agricultural lands that surround it. Accordingly it's a busy, dusty town which, while epitomizing much of modern rural Kenya, still retains that aura of times past that permeates many of the country's towns. See NAIROBI-EXCURSION 3.

Nanyuki: 205 km north of Nairobi. Nanyuki is a major town lying to the west of Mount Kenya (see **A-Z**) and is a good base from which to begin climbs of the mountain or excursions into the national park. Nanyuki stands nearly 2000 m above sea level and lies right on the equator. There are banks, hotels, shops, accommodation and a hospital. See GAME PARKS-MT KENYA.

National Parks & Reserves: There are more than 40 parks and reserves in Kenya with facilities ranging from lodges, camp sites and airstrips to bush and little else. The parks are administered by the Ministry of Tourism and are legally protected from all development other than for tourism and conservation of wildlife, plants and the landscape. Reserves are for the protection of animals but allow a limited range of other activities, usually by local tribespeople. There are also marine parks and reserves (see MOMBASA-EXCURSIONS). Some parks are

more accessible than others and some may be closed periodically due to anti-poaching patrols. The **GAME PARKS** topic of this book offers a selection of some of the best parks and reserves in the country. When visiting parks you should remember a few common-sense rules: drive slowly and carefully, sticking to the tracks; do not wander off on your own (especially on foot!); be careful with fires and take away all litter; make sure you have enough fuel (and water) to at least reach the next place fuel is available; book accommodation in advance; follow the advice of your local guide or driver. See **GAME PARKS**.

Newspapers: There are three daily English-language newspapers: *The Nation*, *The Standard* and the government-controlled *Kenya Times*. They can be obtained throughout the country. In Nairobi and Mombasa you can get a variety of foreign newspapers such as *The Times*, the *Guardian* and *The Herald Tribune*. *Time* and *Newsweek* magazines are both available, though there tend to be distribution problems if there are articles critical of the government. *Taifa Leo* and *Kenya Leo*, both in Swahili, are daily newspapers.

Ngong Hills: The Ngong's overlook Nairobi and stand at 2400 m. They provide excellent views across the city and the plains on either side. See **NAIROBI-EXCURSION 2**.

Nightlife: For most Kenyans nightlife revolves around eating, drinking and dancing. In both Nairobi and Mombasa there is a wide range of places to eat (see **MOMBASA-RESTAURANTS, NAIROBI-RESTAURANTS**) together with a number of clubs and discos (see **NAIROBI-NIGHTLIFE**). On the coast many of the resort hotels organize evening entertainment, while on safari (see **A-Z**) the recommended early-morning start means that eating and going to bed just about covers the evening. The better hotels and lodges will often have videos and/or satellite TV. Most visitors to Kenya will find themselves rediscovering the lost arts of conversation and reading.

Nudism: Generally this is not appreciated, particularly on the coast where the population is predominantly Muslim. Respect their culture and values. If you find a deserted beach around Lamu (see **A-Z**) or elsewhere, then do as you wish but be ready to cover up. Also remember that the tropical sun is stronger than you think (see **Health**).

Nyeri: Standing at 1753 m, Nyeri is the starting point for most visits to the Aberdare National Park (see **GAME PARKS-ABERDARE, Aberdares**). It is an attractive market town for the surrounding coffee-growing farms (see **Coffee**), lying among lush, green hills. Nyeri might also be deemed the capital of the Kikuyu homelands (see **Tribes**) which stretch south to Nairobi and to the east and west. During the Mau Mau (see **A-Z**) it lay right in the heart of the troubles. It is an active, busy spot with a full range of services.

Opening Times: These are fairly constant throughout the country, though with its warmer climate the coast tends to get going slightly earlier in the day and takes longer lunch breaks. Small shops selling basic provisions, often found near the shantytowns and upcountry, can be open at almost any time. Note that many restaurants and clubs do not have fixed opening hours.
Post Offices – 0800-1200, 1400-1630 Mon.-Fri., 0800-1200 Sat.
Banks – 0900-1400 Mon.-Fri., 0900-1100 Sat.
Shops – 0830-1230, 1400-1700 Mon.-Fri., 0830-1230 Sat. There are small variations in these hours depending on the shop and its situation.

Orientation: Kenya lies in East Africa, surrounded by Ethiopia to the north, the Somali Republic and the Indian Ocean to the east, Tanzania to the south and Uganda to the west. Nairobi (see **A-Z**), the capital, lies more or less in the centre of the country and is the main hub for travel to the other regions. Immediately to the north of the city stand the Aberdare Mountains (see **A-Z**) and Mount Kenya (see **A-Z**) and beyond this green mountainous range the land drops away first into savanna and then volcanic desert that stretches up to Lake Turkana (see **A-Z**) and Ethiopia. Running along the western edge of the Aberdares, the Rift Valley (see **A-Z**), with its lakes and volcanoes, splits the country in two. Directly west of Nairobi and over towards the Ugandan border are rolling hills that form the nation's main tea-growing region (see **Tea**). These hills run down to the shores of Lake Victoria (see **A-Z**). South of the capital the terrain falls into low ridges and then dry savanna which sprawls over the border into Tanzania. It is here that Kenya's most famous game parks (see **GAME PARKS**) are to be found. Finally, far to the east across miles of dry grassland lies Mombasa (see **A-Z**) and the coast, a humid tropical strip stretching over 600 km. The topics in this book have been arranged to cover a combination of these geographical areas with the kinds of activity for which Kenya is famous. Accordingly they deal with the game parks, the two major cities of Nairobi and Mombasa and excursions from them to the north, south and west of the country. You're probably as well buying a map of Kenya before you leave home. In Kenya you can purchase reasonable maps of Nairobi and Mombasa, and it's probably worth getting maps of the game parks you are planning to visit if you're not travelling with an organized safari (see **A-Z**).

Passports & Customs: A valid passport is required but not visas for citizens of the UK (except those of Indian or Pakistani origin), Eire, Denmark, The Netherlands, Germany, Spain, Norway, Sweden, Turkey, Italy, Uruguay, Ethiopia and British Commonwealth countries (except Australia, Nigeria and Sri Lanka). Instead you will be granted a visitor's pass for up to three months on arrival. You may be required to show that you have sufficient funds for your stay and an onward ticket. In absence of the latter you may be asked to leave a deposit of £250, refundable on departure. Other nationals, plus those with a South African stamp in their passports, must obtain a visa from a Kenyan embassy or consulate before arrival. Normally travellers coming from South Africa will not be granted entry. You will also be required to complete a currency declaration form on entry (see **Money**). See **Customs Allowances**.

Petrol: Fuel comes in two forms, 'super' and 'regular', and the former should be used in cars. Petrol is widely available in and around towns but once you get out in the bush you may have to plan refuelling stops more carefully. Within the game parks (see GAME PARKS) petrol is available at most of the lodges, though you will have to pay inflated prices. Finally, check your oil and water daily. See **Driving**.

Police: As a visitor to Kenya you are unlikely to have much contact with the police and if you do it's liable to be with members of either the traffic or criminal branches. Roadblocks are fairly common throughout the country though whites are rarely stopped. On the whole they will be willing to advise you if you need information. Nonetheless it is worth mentioning that the police are not well paid, nor on the whole very well educated. Requests for bribes are not unheard of. In whatever circumstances you contact them a friendly, polite manner will get you a lot further than being aggressive. See **Crime & Theft**, **Emergency Number**.

Post Offices: Offices are open 0800-1200, 1400-1630 Mon.-Fri.; 0800-1200 Sat. Parcels can be sent but should be wrapped in brown paper and tied with string. Generally you won't be asked to open them for inspection before sending. Surface mail is considerably cheaper than air mail. Aerogrammes to the UK cost Kshs 3.50, postcards Kshs 4.50. Stamps can be purchased at post offices and stationery and souvenir shops. Letters take four to five days to reach Europe, about a week to the USA. Poste restante services are available in Nairobi, Mombasa, Malindi and Lamu (see **A-Z**). Make sure your name is clearly marked. Mail can also be sent to hotels but should be marked 'For Collection'. You can also receive parcels from home though you may have to negotiate hard if you want to avoid paying import duty on the contents. The main post offices are: Nairobi – currently on Haile Selassie Ave (as the old GPO building on Kenyatta Ave is being renovated); Mombasa – Digo Rd and at the far end of Moi Ave beyond the tusks. Main post offices also offer a telephone and telegram (see **A-Z**) service.

Public Holidays: 1 Jan. (New Year's Day); 1 May (Labour Day); 1 June (Mandaraka Day – commemorating the granting of self-rule in 1960); 20 Oct. (Kenyatta Day – commemorating the imprisonment of Kenyatta – see **A-Z**); 12 Dec. (Jamnihuri/Uhuru Day – Independence celebrations); 25 Dec. (Christmas Day); 26 Dec. (Boxing Day).

Rabies: The disease does exist in Kenya. As a precaution have all animal bites seen to by a doctor (see **Health**).

Railways: Kenya does not have an extensive railway system and the main line runs across the country from Kisumu (see **A-Z**), on Lake Victoria, to the west, through Nairobi to Mombasa in the east. The service to Mombasa runs overnight with trains leaving at 1700 and 1900 and arriving at 0730 and 0800 respectively, and this must be one of the most evocative railway journeys in the world. There are sleeping carriages in first and second class, while third consists of wooden benches; however, second class costs little more than the bus and is extremely good value for money. A delightfully quaint restaurant car serves dinner or if you prefer (or can't afford dinner) white-jacketed stewards will bring sandwiches to your compartment. Men and women are separated into different compartments, unless travelling first class. Although travelling overnight, on the earlier train you would have about an hour's light as you pass through Nairobi National Park (see **NAIROBI-EXCURSION 1**) and across the Athi Plains. This journey is one of the real treats of Kenyan travel and accordingly popular. It's advisable to reserve your seat a day or two in advance and this can be done at the railway station in Nairobi. There is also a line running from Nairobi up past the Aberdares (see **A-Z**) to Nanyuki (see **A-Z**).

Religious Services: Kenya is a multi-faith country. The majority of

the population is Christian (split between Roman Catholic and
Protestant) although there are large numbers of Muslims. The
Independent African Church also has a large following in Nairobi. As a
broad rule of thumb Christianity is predominant in inland areas while
Islam dominates on the coast. Nonetheless, you will find plenty of
mosques and churches in both areas. In addition you'll spot Sikh,
Hindu and Jainist temples. Men, and sometimes women, will be
allowed in the temples as long as they are well-covered and remove
their shoes. English services for Christians are advertised in Sat. editions
of the newspapers (see **A-Z**).

Rift Valley: The Rift Valley in Kenya is the eastern arm of the Great
African Rift which extends from Mozambique in the south to the Red
Sea in the north, a distance of approx. 5000 km. It represents an
attempt by the earth's crust to split into two separate plates, a process
which has been going on for the past 60 million years and which has
resulted in the appearance of several volcanoes in the valley. In Kenya
the rift is some 50 km wide and over 600 m deep. Seeing the valley for
the first time is an incredibly impressive sight as you reach the end of
the escarpment north of Nairobi to see the world drop away below into
this incredible gouge in the earth's surface. See **NAIROBI-EXCURSION 3**.

Safaris: Safari's are generally expensive, whether doing it through a tour company or on your own by hiring a car (see **Car Hire**). That said, the bush and wildlife (see **A-Z**) are one of Kenya's great attractions and a visit to the country is hardly complete without a few days on safari. If going on an organized tour you will have your own driver and the schedule arranged for you. If, however, you drive yourself there are a number of basic rules to be aware of. First and foremost is to note that the wildlife you see is exactly that – wild. You should afford all animals the utmost respect, never getting out of your car, hanging out of windows or the like. Elephant, buffalo and rhino have all been known to charge and likewise lion and cheetah can be unpredictable. Don't make noises to attract the animals' attention, you're far more likely to see their natural behaviour if you're patient and just watch. The game parks are delicate ecosystems subjected to an ever-increasing amount of tourist traffic so heed the signs asking vehicles to stay on the roads. Game wardens are, rightly, increasingly vigilant of tourist excesses. Finally, don't allow your driver, or yourself, to fall into the 'shopping list' trap of rushing round ticking off the animals you should see. Any safari is far more rewarding if you watch, wait and simply enjoy the marvellous scenery and the incredible diversity of wildlife which inhabits it. See GAME PARKS, **National Parks & Reserves**.

Shopping: Most basic everyday items are available in Kenya, though the farther you travel from Nairobi and Mombasa, the more limited the choice becomes. The real fun of shopping in Kenya is to be found at the markets, which is where the real trading goes on. See MOMBASA-SHOPPING, NAIROBI-SHOPPING, **Best Buys**, **Markets**, **Opening Times**.

Smoking: Smoking is still widely accepted in Kenya and there are few restrictions on where you can and cannot smoke.

Sports:
Horse racing – Nairobi racecourse holds meetings most Sun. and is very popular. Its beautiful situation just outside the city makes it a worthwhile excursion for enthusiasts. Race details are printed in the Sun. papers (see **Newspapers**).

Motor racing – the Kenya Safari Rally, held at Easter, is one of the world's most spectacular and gruelling races. It's probably Kenya's sporting highlight of the year. You'll find details of routes and stages in the national press which covers the event comprehensively.

Fishing – see **A-Z**.

Diving – many hotels along the coast offer instruction in scuba diving. Additionally, around the Marine International Parks of Watamu and Malindi (see **A-Z**) and the reefs off Diani (see **MOMBASA-EXCURSION 3**) you will find plenty of operators organizing snorkelling and diving trips.

Windsurfing and boating – most of the coastal hotels have windsurfers for hire. Instruction can be arranged too. Trips out to the reefs in glass-bottomed boats are also widely available.

Swimming – bilharzia (see **Health**) is a real risk in inland rivers and lakes, though Lake Turkana (see **A-Z**) is safe. On the coast there are few problems, although the surf can be surprisingly strong. Sharks and the like do not come inside the reefs.

Golf – there are several good golf clubs in Nairobi, namely Muthaiga Golf Club, Royal Nairobi Golf Club, Sigona Golf Club and at the Limuru Country Club. All offer temporary membership.

Taxis: Taxis are plentiful, especially in Nairobi and Mombasa. Few have meters so agree a price before your journey, so as not to have a nasty and expensive surprise at the end. As with other purchases bargain hard. The two most reliable companies are Kenatco and the yellow-banded municipal taxis. For longer journeys there are Peugeot taxis operating between the main towns, and normally you'll find yourself sharing the ride with others. See **Tipping**.

Tea: Tea is an important export crop in Kenya and the country is one of the world's biggest exporters of tea (third after India and Sri Lanka). The main area of tea production is around Kericho, in western Kenya (see **NAIROBI–EXCURSION 4**), where there is the optimum combination of climate (high rainfall but also sunshine) and landscape. As with coffee, much of the country's tea is now grown on smallholdings.

Telephones & Telegrams: Public telephones can be used for local calls and are relatively plentiful in towns. There are easy-to-follow instructions for use inside. For international calls you can 'phone from your hotel (although this is slightly more expensive); these calls will be placed through the operator. Direct dialling is possible from private telephones; dial 000, the country code (e.g. UK 44, USA 1), followed by the area code (minus the zero) and finally the number. Otherwise, international calls need to be made from a post office (see **A-Z**). Calls are paid for in advance with a refund if you fail to get through. Accordingly it's wise to make person-to-person rather than station-to-station calls. It's cheaper to 'phone abroad between 1800-0600. The area codes for Nairobi and Mombasa are 2 and 11 respectively. Telegrams can be sent through the telephone operator.

Television & Radio: Voice of Kenya Radio broadcasts in English from 0600-2300. With a short wave radio you can pick up the BBC World Service, Voice of America and other international services. Voice of Kenya also operates the national TV station which broadcasts in a combination of English and Swahili. Much of the programming is imported. KTN is a newly-established cable network broadcasting news and films. Videos are very popular in Kenya and many hotels are equipped with recorders and a selection of films.

Thesiger, Wilfred (1910-): One of the world's great travel writers of today has a house in the town of Maralal (see **NAIROBI–EXCURSION 5**). Thesiger started his career in the Colonial Service in the Sudan and was later to serve with the SAS in the Western Desert during World War II. He went on to spend years in the marshlands of southern Iraq and Iran and the deserts of the Empty Quarter of Oman and Saudi Arabia, before returning once more to Africa.

Time Difference: Kenya is 3 hr ahead of GMT all year round.

Tipping: Many hotels and restaurants will include a service charge on the bill so tipping the waiter is at your discretion. 10% is considered quite reasonable. Giving Kshs 5 or 10 to people who help you by carrying bags or giving directions always goes down well and will often smooth your passage. On safari you should tip your driver well, increasing the tip with the number of days you've spent with him. This could rise to as much as Kshs 600-700.

Toilets: Hotels and restaurants have the necessary facilities, though of widely varying standards depending on the establishment. Public toilets are rare and only recommended if you have a nasal blockage and sturdy shoes; they tend to be of the 'squat' variety.

Tourist Information: While there are tourist information offices in Nairobi, on Kenyatta Ave, and in Mombasa, on Moi Ave, they are of fairly limited help. Generally you'll get the best information from tour operators, hotel staff and fellow travellers. The Kenyan Tourist Office, 25 Brooksmills, London, W1Y 1LG, tel: 071-3553144, may be of help.

Tours: See **Guides**, **Safaris**.

Transport: See **Buses**, **Car Hire**, **Matatus**, **Railways**, **Taxis**.

Traveller's Cheques: See **Money**.

Treetops: The hotel was built in a tree in the Aberdares in 1932. It first came to international prominence in 1952 when Princess Elizabeth was staying there and acceded to the throne on her father's death. The original hotel was burnt down in 1955 and was rebuilt on stilts and on a larger scale. At night hoards of wildlife are drawn to the water hole which the hotel overlooks, providing unforgettable game viewing. Yet for many its the experience of staying in the wooden tree house steeped

in history that makes the visit. See **GAME PARKS-ABERDARE**.

Tribes: There are estimated to be more than 40 tribal groupings in
Kenya. Since independence the government has been active in promot-
ing a Kenyan national identity, and discouraging the tribalism which
had been sustained as a means of colonial control. While intermarriage
continues to merge tribal distinctions there are perhaps five groupings
that the visitor is most likely to encounter:

Masai – probably the best known of East Africa's tribes, the Masai are
today predominantly found in the area between Nairobi and the
Tanzanian border. Currently numbering some 250,000 they are readily
identifiable by their height and fine features. You will see them guard-
ing their cattle with long spears and dressed in cloaks. They have tend-
ed to resist the modernizing influences of today's Kenya and remain
proudly independent. They were once the most feared warriors in the
country.

Samburu – closely related to the Masai, the Samburu inhabit the lands
north of the Aberdares (see **A-Z**) and south of Lake Turkana (see **A-Z**).
The young men are a particularly impressive sight with their long
ochre-stained hair.

Turkana – historically another extremely warlike tribe, they are found in
the areas surrounding Lake Turkana. The Turkana were also cattle
herders who, like the Masai, were much famed for their diet of milk
and blood (tapped from veins in a cow's neck). In recent times they
have turned more to fishing the rich depths of Lake Turkana.

Luo – the Luo are the second-largest tribe in Kenya, numbering over
two-and-a-half million. The area around Lake Victoria (see **A-Z**) is their
homeland where, historically, they have been fishermen and agricultur-
alists. Close and enthusiastic association with missionary schools have
earned the Luo a reputation as the country's academics. They have
largely assimilated into the ways of modern Kenya.

Kikuyu – the Kikuyu homelands are the highlands north of Nairobi
stretching through the Aberdares and Mount Kenya (see **A-Z**).
Numbering over seven million they are Kenya's biggest tribal grouping
and as such have played a prominent role in the country's recent development. Kenya's first President, Jomo Kenyatta (see **A-Z**), was from the

Kikuyu tribe, though he always regarded tribalism as a national scourge. The Kikuyu were also much used by the British in their administration of the country, which added to the tribe's influence. Today their numbers and commercial acumen ensure they remain an important political force in the country.

Uhuru: Means 'freedom' in Swahili and and was the cry of nationalists up to independence. Today it retains that same meaning.

What's On: For local information the national newspapers usually carry information about events throughout the country. Most travel agents and good hotels in Kenya have free copies of *What's On; Tourist Guide To Kenya*, published monthly, which contains a great deal of information covering the whole country with street maps and details of various activities, hotels, restaurants and game parks. See **Newspapers**.

Wildlife: Kenya has an incredible variety of wildlife of which only the most common animals are covered here. For those who want more information there are plenty of books on the subject. See for instance, *A Field Guide to the National Parks of East Africa* by J. G. Williams and N. Arlott (HarperCollins). You will also find that guides and game park staff are both helpful and knowledgeable. Remember that however familiar and tame the animals appear, they are wild. Most can cause severe injury so treat them with caution and respect.
Elephant (*Tembo*) – found both out in open bush and in the forests of the Aberdares (see **A–Z**). They live in herds so if you see one others are almost sure to be close by. The African elephant differs from the Indian elephant in several ways, but is most noticeably larger.
Rhinoceros (*Kifaru*) – this is one of the rarer animals to spot on safari due to its solitary nature and tendency to feed in shoulder-high bush. Although not a carnivore it should be treated with some respect. The more common black rhino is most likely to be found in Amboseli or the Masai Mara. The much rarer white rhino can be found in Tsavo though poaching has culled its numbers dramatically. It's not actually white but has a rather more prominent jaw than its black counterpart.
Hippopotamus (*Kiboko*) – found in rivers throughout Kenya, most game

parks have a 'hippo pool' where you're most likely to see just the nostrils and ears of these bulky animals. They remain in the water during the day and come ashore at night to graze. Trails through the undergrowth mark their routes to and from the rivers, something to be aware of if you're camping (see **A-Z**). Hippos are part of the pig family and despite weighing in at well over two tonnes they can run faster than a human.

Lion (*Simba*) – roam the open grasslands in prides made up of a number of females, cubs and one male. They hunt at dawn and dusk but only when hungry. Working as a team the females stalk zebra, wildebeest, gazelle and buffalo, identifying the weakest before moving in for the kill. They will also steal from other predators. After feeding they become very lethargic, lazing around in the sun. Don't be misled, however cuddly and tame they appear, as lions can be extremely dangerous.

Cheetah (*Duma*) – renowned as the fastest mammal in the world, they can achieve 100 kph in short sprints. The cheetah is found in open scrubland, often in groups.

Leopard (*Chui*) – looks very similar to the cheetah though its head is larger and its spots are grouped in patterns. They also tend to be slightly smaller and wirier. They live around cliffs and rocks and hunt at night, making them a rare sighting for the visitor. However, some of the game lodges hang meat out at night to draw them into floodlit areas.

Hyena (*Fisi*) – the spotted hyena hunts in large packs and despite their

reputation as scavengers they do sometimes kill their own prey. You're most likely to see them fighting over an old carcass. About the size of a dog, their hunchbacks and cackling howl have made them, perhaps unfairly, one of the most disliked of African wildlife.

Crocodile (*Mamba*) – lives in both rivers and lakes and can be incredibly tricky to spot, though you may be lucky and find them sunning themselves on the shore. If camping near water it's wise to be aware of their possible presence. Some of the game lodges put out meat to attract them onto the banks as an evening entertainment for their guests.

Zebra (*Punda Milia*) – found throughout Kenya in large herds that are often mixed with wildebeest, giraffe and antelope. The size of a horse, they are the favourite prey of the predatory population. There are two types of zebra, the common variety and Grevy's zebra, which is slightly larger and has thinner stripes.

Wildebeest (*Nyumbu*) – also called gnu, you're likely to see these in greater abundance than almost any other species. They look ridiculous with their clumsy, over-long legs, shaggy mane, rather vacant look and cud-chewing mouths. Vast herds migrate through the Serengeti Plains in Tanzania into Kenya each year – this has to be one of the most spectacular sights the animal kingdom has to offer. Wildebeest are another favourite prey of the predators.

Grant's Gazelle (*Swala Granti*) – a slim graceful antelope with backward-curving horns. They are tan-coloured with a white backside and belly, and a dark-brown stripe down the face. They are found in open grassland.

Thomson's Gazelle (*Swala Tommi*) – very similar to the Grant's Gazelle, it is more reddy-brown and has an identifying black streak along both flanks.

Impala (*Swala Pala*) – dark brown in colour, the impala lives in large herds in bushy scrubland. They are most easily spotted by their tendency to jump athletically into the air whenever alarmed.

Dikdik (*Dikdiki*) – a tiny antelope standing just over 0.3 m tall, the dikdik has a grey-brown coat and long snout. They live in pairs and are most often spotted grazing between thornbushes.

Eland (*Pofu*) – this is the biggest of the antelopes and is easily identified by its size and the twisted horns found on both male and females. They live in herds on open grassland and can often be seen intermingled with other herds of zebra and wildebeest.

Oryx (*Choroa*) – another large antelope standing 1.2 m high with long straight horns and a reddy-brown hide. You're most likely to see them in Tsavo and Amboseli.

Bushbuck (*Pongo*) – the bushbuck is a shy creature that lives in small groups in forested terrain. It has delicate, almost striped markings and a white belly.

Waterbuck (*Kuro*) – a large antelope which, as its name suggests, is most commonly found near water. They live in herds led by a dominant male and can be found around Amboseli and Tsavo and again near the coast. They have dull-brown coats, a white backside and longer hair than most other antelope.

Giraffe (*Twiga*) – generally found on open grassland feeding off trees, particularly the acacia. Although the tallest mammals, standing 5.5 m tall and weighing over a tonne, these are shy creatures and your approach may well send them off into their strange rocking gait. You may also spot just a head and neck peering at you from behind a tree.

Buffalo (*Nyati*) – found both on open grassland and in thick bush the buffalo is one of the most feared of African animals. Don't be misled by their bovine appearance; they are extremely bad-tempered and powerful, and account for more injuries and deaths than any other animal in Kenya. They live in herds and feed off grass.

Warthog (*Ngiri*) – small ugly pig-like animals with warts on their snouts and short tusks. They live both in forests and in scrubland in small groups. When alarmed their tales point straight up in the air in apprehension.

Ostrich (*Mbuni*) – found on the open plains of Kenya often intermixed with herds of antelope. They stand nearly 2.5 m high and although they can't fly they can run at speeds of around 25 kph. It's true that they will sometimes stick their heads in the ground when approached. Again beware; their powerful kick can kill.

Baboon (*Nyani Mkubwa*) – this large monkey with its long snout and shaggy mane lives mostly on the ground in large troops led by a dominant male. They sleep in trees at night. They are scavengers who will eat virtually anything and when camping they can be something of a nuisance. Make sure you keep all movables and eatables shut in your vehicle.

Colobus Monkey (*Mbega*) – lives in mountain forests and is most likely to be seen in the Aberdares. They are black with a white mane, face and bushy tail.

Sykes' Monkey (*Kima*) – found mostly in forests this dark-grey monkey with black arms and legs is a fruit-eater. They are surprisingly friendly and on picnics you may find yourself with an audience.

See GAME PARKS, **National Parks & Reserves**.

Youth Hostels: Kenya has very few youth hostels but there are some in Nairobi, Mombasa and at Mount Kenya (see **A-Z**). In Nairobi the

hostel is at Ralph Bunche Rd (take bus 34 from the airport). The hostel is not very central and you should be careful when going down into the city – take a bus or walk down the main road rather than cutting through the park as there have been incidents of mugging in the park, even in broad daylight. If you are not already a member you will have to join the association before you can stay. There are also YMCAs in Nairobi, Mombasa, Kisumu and, most popular of all, at Lake Naivasha (see **A-Z**). The youth hostels are inexpensive, but they are also very busy so it is best to book ahead.

This book was produced using QuarkXPress™
and Adobe Illustrator 88™ on Apple
Macintosh™ computers and output to separated
film on a Linotronic™ 300 Imagesetter

Text: Craig Swan
Photography: Alan Lavender Photography
Electronic Cartography: Susan Harvey Design

First published 1992
Copyright © HarperCollins Publishers
Published by HarperCollins Publishers
Printed in Hong Kong
ISBN 0 00 435849-X